Student Activity Guide

Housing

. . . .

D E C I S I O N S

by
Claudia Dufek Lazok
High School Administrator
Tuscon Unified School District
and
Evelyn L. Lewis
Professor Emeritus, Home Economics
Northern Arizona University
Flagstaff, Arizona

Publisher
The Goodheart-Willcox Company, Inc.
Tinley Park, Illinois

Introduction

. . . .

This activity guide is designed for use with the text *Housing Decisions*. It will help you recall and review concepts presented in the text. It will also help you to understand your housing needs and will allow you to evaluate various housing alternatives.

The best way to use this activity guide is to begin by reading your assignment in the text. You will find that the activities in this guide correspond to the chapters in the text. Follow the instructions carefully at the beginning of each activity.

Do your best to complete these activities carefully and accurately. Try to complete as much of each activity as you can without referring to the text. Then compare the answers you have to the information in *Housing Decisions*. At that time you can also complete any questions you could not answer.

Other activities will ask for opinions, evaluations, and conclusions that cannot be judged as right or wrong. The goal of these activities is to encourage you to consider alternatives and evaluate situations thoughtfully. The text will be a useful reference in completing these activities.

The activities in this guide have been designed to be interesting and fun. They will help you apply what you have learned as you make housing decisions of your own, now and in the future.

Copyright 2000
by
The Goodheart-Willcox Company, Inc.
Previous Editions Copyright 1994, 1987, 1984

International Standard Book Number 1-56637-652-1

3 4 5 6 7 8 9 10 00 05 04 03 02 01

Table of Contents

Part 6 Progress in Housing

• •

Housing and Human Needs

Human Needs

Activity A   Name _____

Chapter 1   Date _____ Period _____

Complete the pyramid of Maslow's priority of human needs. Explain each need and describe ways in which housing can help to fulfill them.

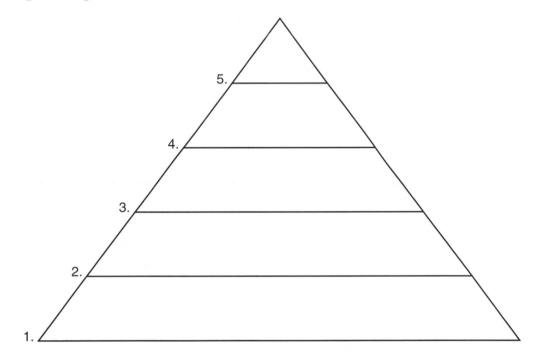

1. Need: _____ Explanation: _____

   Ways in which housing can fulfill this need:_____

2. Need: _____ Explanation: _____

   Ways in which housing can fulfill this need:_____

3. Need: _____ Explanation: _____

   Ways in which housing can fulfill this need:_____

4. Need: _____ Explanation: _____

   Ways in which housing can fulfill this need:_____

5. Need: _____ Explanation: _____

   Ways in which housing can fulfill this need:_____

Space and Privacy Needs

Activity B   Name _____

Chapter 1   Date _____ Period _____

Working with three or four classmates, compare factors that affect people's space and privacy needs. Each group member should interview a person, using the Interview Questions below. (No more than one person should be interviewed in each of the age categories listed.) Report your findings to the group and answer the Discussion Questions that follow.

Interview Questions

1. Which category includes your age?

   _____ 5-10 _____ 11-16 _____ 17-21 _____ 22-30 _____ 31-45 _____ 46-60 _____ over 60

2. How many people live in your home? _____

3. What is the smallest size home in which you would feel comfortable? _____

4. Why? _____

5. What rooms, areas, or objects in your home do you consider part of your private space? _____
   _____

6. Why? _____
   _____

7. How do you spend time in your private space? _____
   _____
   _____

8. What problems have you had in keeping your private space to yourself? _____
   _____
   _____
   _____

Discussion Questions

1. How does age affect people's space and privacy needs? _____
   _____
   _____

2. How do hobbies and interests affect people's space and privacy needs? _____
   _____
   _____

3. How does the value of family unity affect people's space needs? _____
   _____
   _____

Your Housing Needs and Values

Name _____

Date _____ Period _____

In the space below, clip and mount a picture of a room that reflects your values, or draw your ideal room.

List three needs addressed by the room in the above picture, and indicate if each is physical or psychological in nature. Identify a value associated with each need.

Need	Value

Living Units

Name _____

Date _____ Period _____

Draw or clip and mount two different cartoon examples of living units. For each, identify the living un[it] shown (one-person, single-parent family, nuclear family, or extended family). Describe how th[e] characters fit into the living unit.

Living unit: _____

Description: _____

_____

_____

_____

Living unit: _____

Description: _____

_____

_____

_____

Family Life Cycles

Name _____

Date _____ Period _____

Complete the illustration below by listing the substages of the family life cycle. Then describe how each stage affects housing needs.

Beginning Stage	Expanding Stage	Developing Stage	Launching Stage	Aging Stage
		Substages		
_____	_____	_____	_____	_____
_____	_____	_____	_____	_____
_____	_____	_____	_____	_____
_____	_____	_____	_____	_____
_____	_____	_____	_____	_____
_____	_____	_____	_____	_____

1. Housing needs of the beginning stage: _____
_____
_____

2. Housing needs of the expanding stage: _____
_____
_____

3. Housing needs of the developing stage: _____
_____
_____

4. Housing needs of the launching stage: _____
_____
_____

5. Housing needs of the aging stage: _____
_____
_____

Family Stages

Name _____

Date _____ Period _____

Interview one or two members of a family to learn about its housing needs. Then answer the questions that follow.

1. What are the ages of the family members living at home as well as away from home? _____

    _____

    _____

    _____

    _____

    _____

    _____

    _____

    _____

2. In what stage of the family life cycle is this family? Explain. _____

    _____

    _____

3. In what substage(s) of the family life cycle is this family? _____

    _____

    Explain. _____

    _____

    _____

4. What are the present housing needs of this family? _____

    _____

    _____

    _____

    _____

5. How might this family's housing needs change in the future? _____

    _____

    _____

    _____

    _____

    _____

    _____

    _____

Lifestyles

Name _____

Date _____ Period _____

In the space provided, clip and mount two housing advertisements that reflect different lifestyles. Identify and describe each lifestyle represented. List your opinion of their advantages and disadvantages.

Lifestyle: _____

Description: _____

_____

_____

_____

Advantages: _____

_____

_____

_____

Disadvantages: _____

_____

_____

_____

Lifestyle: _____

Description: _____

_____

_____

_____

_____

Advantages: _____

_____

_____

Disadvantages: _____

_____

_____

_____

Human Needs and Housing Crossword Puzzle

Activity H

Chapter 1

Name _____

Date _____ Period _____

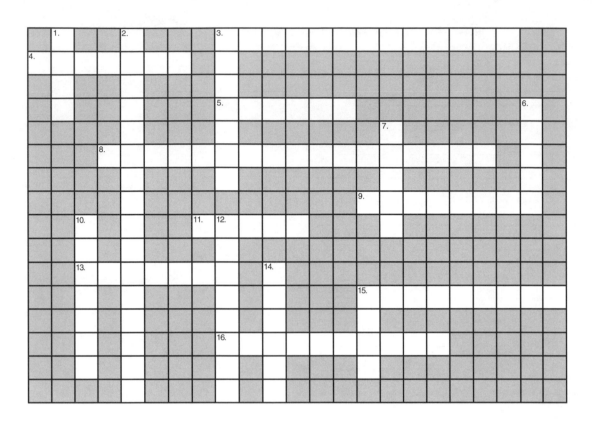

Across

3. Security and self-esteem are _____ needs.
4. _____ refers to the dwelling and all that is within and near it.
5. You use your personal _____ when you choose between two or more things.
8. The highest level of human need is _____-_____, or the fulfillment of your potential.
9. _____ is a psychological need for protection from the outside world.
11. _____ is needed to prevent feeling crowded.
13. The value reflected when emphasis is placed on the cost of housing is _____.
15. A living pattern or way of life is called _____.
16. _____ is the ability to create in imaginative ways.

Down

1. One of the basic physical needs is _____.
2. Your housing environment is called you_____.
3. The need to be where others cannot see and hear what you are doing is _____.
6. An area designed for group living show the value of family _____.
7. Besides food, a basic physical need require for survival is _____.
10. A basic need provided by housing is _____
12. _____ needs is the category of human need basic to everyone.
14. High regard from others is _____.
15. _____ and acceptance, also known a belonging, is a higher need than security.

Influences on Housing

Housing in My Community

Activity A   Name_____

Chapter 2   Date_____ Period _____

Invite a city planner and/or local historian to visit the class and discuss the growth of the community. Ask questions regarding the following topics. In the space provided, summarize the speaker's comments.

Recent residential growth (in general): _____

_____

_____

_____

_____

Transportation and highways: _____

_____

_____

_____

Commercial, industrial, or business growth: _____

_____

_____

_____

Housing needs: _____

_____

_____

_____

Housing industry and current projects:_____

_____

_____

_____

_____

Groups concerned with housing needs: _____

_____

_____

Groups concerned with the environment:_____

_____

Culture and Society Influence Housing

Activity B

Chapter 2

Name _____

Date _____ Period _____

Read the cultural and societal factors listed below. In the space provided, describe the effects of eac factor on housing.

Cultural/Societal Factors

Influence on Housing

1. The Navajo believed that spirit guardians need a place to enter the house.

1. _____
   _____

2. Europeans desired home ownership.

2. _____
   _____

3. Old Spanish missions were preserved.

3. _____
   _____

4. Various cultures came from Europe.

4. _____
   _____

5. Household size has decreased.

5. _____
   _____

6. There are increased numbers of single adults, many of whom choose to live alone.

6. _____
   _____

7. The number of people in the over-65 age group is increasing.

7. _____
   _____

8. People with disabilities are members of living units.

8. _____
   _____

9. Many people live on fixed incomes.

9. _____
   _____

10. Many women are employed outside the home.

10. _____
    _____

11. Many people enjoy spending their leisure time at home.

11. _____
    _____

12. Today's society is very mobile.

12. _____
    _____

Housing Environments

Name _____

Date _____ Period _____

omplete the following exercises on housing environments.

art 1: For these ten items, place one letter in each blank as follows: **N** if the term describes the natural environment; **C** if the term describes the constructed environment; and **B** if the term describes the behavioral environment.

_____	1. Intelligence	_____	6. Anger
_____	2. Land	_____	7. Human energy
_____	3. House	_____	8. Air conditioner
_____	4. Attitude	_____	9. Happiness
_____	5. Solar energy	_____	10. Water

art 2: Look through current newspapers and magazines. Clip and mount an article or picture of each of the following environments. Using descriptive words, explain how each of these articles or pictures relates to the housing environment.

xample of natural environment:

/ays in which this relates to the housing environment: _____

_____

_____

_____

_____

_____

_____

(Continued)

Example of constructed environment:

Ways in which this relates to the housing environment: _____

_____

_____

_____

Example of behavioral environment:

Ways in which this relates to the housing environment: _____

_____

_____

_____

Give an example of how one type of environment can overlap another type. _____

_____

_____

_____

Housing and the Economy

Name _____

Date _____ Period _____

In the space provided, mount a picture of a house from a brochure or catalog. Then list all the jobs that may have been involved in building, selling, furnishing, and decorating the house. You may want to look through the *Dictionary of Occupational Titles* or another resource that lists various jobs to help you find those related to housing.

Jobs involved in building this house:	Jobs involved in selling this house:	Jobs involved in furnishing and decorating this house:
_____	_____	_____
_____	_____	_____
_____	_____	_____
_____	_____	_____
_____	_____	_____
_____	_____	_____
_____	_____	_____
_____	_____	_____
_____	_____	_____
_____	_____	_____
_____	_____	_____

Filling a House with High Tech

Activity E

Chapter 2

Name_____

Date_____ Period _____

In the space provided, mount pictures of high tech products that are available for use in the rooms listed.
Explain how these products can improve the quality of housing.

```
                    ┌─┐
                   ╱│ │╲
                  ╱ │ │ ╲
                 ╱  └─┘  ╲
                ╱  BEDROOM │ BATHROOM ╲
               ╱           │           ╲
              │            │            │
              │            │            │
              │            │            │
              │  KITCHEN   │   LIVING ROOM │
              │            │            │
              │            │            │
              └────────────┴────────────┘
```

These products can improve housing the following ways:

Bedroom:_____

_____

_____

Bathroom: _____

_____

_____

Kitchen: _____

_____

_____

Living room:_____

_____

_____

Using Decision-Making Skills

Thought Involved in Making Decisions

Activity A   Name _____

Chapter 3   Date _____ Period _____

Complete the following exercises on decisions.

Case 1—Decorating Decisions

1. The color and style of the draperies in the living room need to be changed to coordinate with the new furnishings recently purchased. You shop until you find the exact color and style of draperies. What type of decision have you made? _____

2. While in a wallpaper shop looking for a design to match the fabric swatches for the bedroom, you see a pattern that could be used in the bathroom. You purchase the rolls needed to paper the bathroom without a thought about how it would look. What type of decision have you made?

   _____

3. In which decision were the consequences considered? _____

   _____

4. In which decision was little thought given to possible outcomes? _____

   _____

5. What are some possible negative outcomes of each decision? _____

   _____

   _____

6. Which decision is likely to give you more long-term satisfaction? _____

   _____

Case 2—Wake-Up Decisions

7. Your alarm rings on a weekday morning. You turn off the alarm, go into the bathroom, and turn on the shower. What type of decision have you made? _____

8. What are some possible advantages of this type of decision? _____

   _____

   _____

9. What are some possible disadvantages of this type of decision?_____

   _____

   _____

10. What events could occur when you turn on the shower that would change the type of decision made?

   _____

   _____

   _____

Decision Groupings

Name _____

Date _____ Period _____

Read the following paragraph. Then diagram a possible chain decision and a possible central satellite decision based on the information provided. (You may make your own assumptions about any information that is not provided. Both decisions may be based on the same or different assumptions.)

> The Benson family always uses the municipal pool in town for swimming in the summer, but the city has decided to close the pool. The Bensons don't want to stop summertime swimming, so they must decide on an alternative. They have many options. They could join a private pool in the area for about three times the cost of the city municipal pool. They could use the municipal pool in the next city at a slightly higher cost, but more time would be spent traveling to and from the pool. The Bensons could buy a pool for their backyard. The initial cost could be very high depending on the type of pool purchased. However, money would be saved in pool memberships, and the pool would be very convenient.

The Bensons might decide on the following chain of decisions:

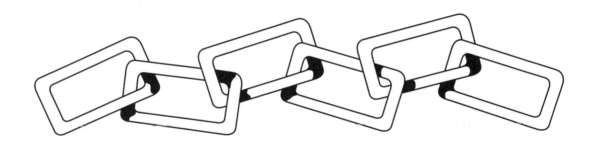

The Bensons might decide on the following group of central-satellite decisions:

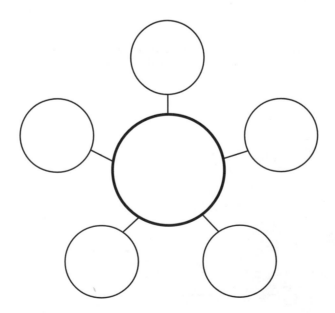

Resources

Name_____

Date_____ Period _____

eparate the following list of resources into human and nonhuman resources.

Ambition	Friends	Photographic memory
Car	High energy level	Savings
Coordination	House	Telephone
Creativity	Library	Time
Employment	Math skills	Tools and equipment
Excellent health	Money	Positive attitude

Human resources:

1. _____
2. _____
3. _____
4. _____
5. _____
6. _____
7. _____
8. _____
9. _____

Nonhuman resources:

1. _____
2. _____
3. _____
4. _____
5. _____
6. _____
7. _____
8. _____
9. _____

ist 15 community resources near your home.

1. _____
2. _____
3. _____
4. _____
5. _____
6. _____
7. _____
8. _____
9. _____
0. _____
1. _____
2. _____
3. _____
4. _____
5. _____

Human Resources

Name _____

Date _____ Period _____

Assess the human resources of two families you know, using the inventory chart below. Rate each family member on a scale of 0 (poor) to 10 (good). Then analyze their ratings by answering the questions and following the directions on the next page.

Inventory of Human Resources

Human Resources	Physical health	Energy	Knowledge and information	Ability or skill	Attitude	Other (specify)
Family 1						
Husband/Father:						
Wife/Mother:						
Teenagers: (1)						
(2)						
Children: (1)						
(2)						
Others: (1)						
(2)						
Total members:						
Family 2						
Husband/Father:						
Wife/Mother:						
Teenagers: (1)						
(2)						
Children: (1)						
(2)						
Others: (1)						
(2)						
Total members:						

(Continued

1. Judging from their scores, which family do you think would be better able to handle a do-it-your-self remodeling project? Why?

   _____
   _____
   _____
   _____
   _____
   _____

2. Consider the family that is not as skillful to handle the project. What additional resources (either human or nonhuman) could this family use to have a successful remodeling project? Explain how each additional resource would be helpful.

   _____
   _____
   _____
   _____
   _____
   _____

3. For both families, write which family member you think would be best suited to handle the following tasks.

	Family 1	**Family 2**
• Making arrangements with a remodeling contractor:	_____	_____
• Carrying supplies into the house:	_____	_____
• Providing moral support:	_____	_____
• Cleaning paintbrushes:	_____	_____

4. Describe how taking an inventory of human resources can be helpful to a family.

   _____
   _____
   _____
   _____
   _____
   _____
   _____
   _____

Decision Making

Name _____

Date _____ Period _____

Solve a housing problem by using the decision-making steps below.

1. State the problem. _____

_____

_____

_____

_____

2. Find the causes of the problem. _____

_____

_____

_____

_____

_____

3. Consider the effects of the problem. _____

_____

_____

_____

_____

_____

4. List alternative solutions to the problem. _____

_____

_____

_____

_____

_____

5. What resources will be needed to solve this problem? _____

_____

_____

_____

_____

_____

(Continued

6. What are the consequences of each solution? _____

_____

_____

_____

_____

_____

_____

_____

_____

_____

7. Will the outcome give lasting satisfaction? _____

8. Will everyone involved be satisfied? _____

9. What other decisions must be made? _____

_____

_____

_____

_____

_____

_____

_____

10. Which alternative will be chosen and what necessary action must be taken? _____

_____

_____

_____

_____

_____

_____

_____

_____

_____

_____

Resources and Decisions

Name _____

Date _____ Period _____

Complete the following sentences by placing the missing word(s) in the preceding blanks.

_____ 1. A(n) _____ decision is a type of decision where consequences are considered and choices are made only after looking at problems carefully.

_____ 2. _____-_____-_____-_____ decisions are made hurriedly with little thought given to possible outcomes.

_____ 3. _____ _____ is action that results from habit.

_____ 4. _____ decisions create other choices that must be made to complete the action.

_____ 5. A _____-_____ decision is a major decision surrounded by related, but independent, decisions.

_____ 6. _____ are sources of supply or support.

_____ 7. When you use your ability, knowledge, or energy, you are using a _____ resource.

_____ 8. _____ resources include property, money, goods, and excellent neighborhood transportation.

_____ 9. The public library, city parks, hospitals, the police department, schools, and shopping centers are _____ resources.

_____ 10. If you know how to fix your toaster, you have _____ as a resource.

_____ 11. If you are willing to take a difficult course that you know will benefit you in the future, you have the resource of a good _____.

_____ 12. People who play sports in their free time and do manual labor at their jobs have a high _____ level.

_____ 13. _____ is the only resource that all people have in equal amounts.

_____ 14. The resource of _____ is needed to buy or rent housing.

_____ 15. Land, buildings, and furnishings are _____ resources.

_____ 16. Stating the problem, finding the causes, and considering the effects are steps in the decision-making process called _____.

_____ 17. When the decision-making process is used, the members of the living unit are more likely to receive _____.

· ·

Choosing a Place to Live

Your Community Zoning Rules

Activity A   Name _____

Chapter 4   Date _____ Period _____

Invite a member of a zoning authority or the city council to present information about zoning rules in your community. Record the information in the space provided.

1. List zoning rules that have been established in your community within the last five years. _____

_____

_____

_____

_____

_____

_____

_____

_____

_____

2. Are there any zoning rules that are presently being considered for change? If so, describe them.

_____

_____

_____

_____

3. Who makes the decisions regarding zoning rules? _____

_____

4. What is the procedure used to establish new zoning rules? _____

_____

_____

_____

(Continued)

5. How are zoning rules carried out and enforced? _____

_____

_____

_____

_____

_____

_____

_____

6. If a citizen feels that a zoning rule is being violated, what action can he or she take? _____

_____

_____

_____

_____

_____

_____

_____

7. What happens when members of the community are opposed to the zoning rules being considered for adoption? _____

_____

_____

_____

_____

_____

_____

8. Describe any conflicts in the community about present zoning rules. _____

_____

_____

_____

_____

_____

_____

_____

Evaluating a Place to Live

Activity B

Chapter 4

Name _____

Date _____ Period _____

Visit a subdivision. Walk through the models and complete the following evaluation.

Name of subdivision: _____

Check off the areas below that best describe this subdivision.

Site size:

_____ Large

_____ Medium

_____ Small

Site shape:

_____ Regular

_____ Irregular

Contour of the land:

_____ Level

_____ Gentle slope

_____ Steep slope

Soil characteristics:

_____ Sand

_____ Gravel

_____ Rock

_____ Clay

Lots:

_____ Attractive

_____ Unattractive

Location in community:

_____ Edge

_____ Center

Traffic:

_____ Much street traffic

_____ Little street traffic

Type of structures:

_____ Single-family

_____ Multifamily

_____ Mixed

Density of population:

_____ Sparse

_____ Crowded

Neighborhood:

_____ Residential

_____ Commercial

_____ Industrial

_____ Combination

Population composition:

_____ Homogeneous (similar)

_____ Heterogeneous (varied)

Recreational facilities:

_____ Park and/or play areas

_____ No park or play areas

Describe the structural quality of the homes. _____

_____

How far are the nearest grocery store and shopping center? _____

How far is the nearest school? _____

How far is the nearest medical facility? _____

How far is the nearest recreational facility? _____

How far is the nearest fire department? _____

How far is the nearest police department? _____

What are the advantages of this subdivision? _____

_____

What are the disadvantages of this subdivision? _____

Housing Location

Name _____

Date _____ Period _____

On the next page, design a site and neighborhood for the house shown below. Include the following i
the neighborhood sketch: streets, the shapes of the lots, and an arrow placed near the house marke
North to indicate direction. After completing the neighborhood sketch, provide answers to the question
and statements on this page. Share your design with the class.

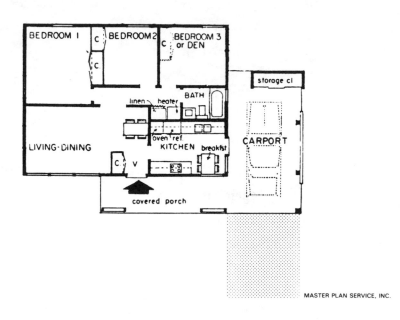

MASTER PLAN SERVICE, INC.

1. In which direction does the house face? Why? _____

_____

_____

2. Describe the lot design. _____

_____

3. Describe the placement of the streets. _____

_____

4. Is the lot size appropriate for this house? Why? _____

_____

5. What community resources would you place near this neighborhood? Why? _____

_____

_____

6. What community resources would you place away from this neighborhood? Why? _____

_____

_____

(Continue

Creating Site Zones

Name _____

Date _____ Period _____

Sketch a lot design around the house floor plan below. You may wish to include landscape walls, fence trees, shrubs, and hedges in your design. Identify the zones within the site using the following colors

Public zone = red

Service zone = yellow

Private zone = blue

The public zone includes these areas:

_____

_____

The service zone includes these areas:

_____

_____

The private zone includes these areas:

_____

_____

Choices

Name _____

Date _____ Period _____

ind and list businesses that supply each of the housing choices listed below. Use the classified section f the local newspaper and a local telephone directory to find the businesses. Then answer the questions hat follow.

uilder, custom-designed homes:

• _____

• _____

ondominium units:

• _____

• _____

ooperative units:

• _____

• _____

1anufactured housing:

• _____

• _____

1obile homes:

• _____

• _____

Modular houses:

1. _____

2. _____

Rental apartments:

1. _____

2. _____

Rental houses:

1. _____

2. _____

Rental trucks/trailers for do-it-yourself moving:

1. _____

2. _____

Professional movers:

1. _____

2. _____

Vhich of the above housing styles do you prefer? Why?

_____

_____

_____

Vhich of the above housing styles do you dislike? Why?

_____

_____

_____

you were moving, would you use a professional mover or do it yourself? Why?

_____

_____

_____

Special Housing Needs

Name _____

Date _____ Period _____

Interview a person with a physical disability, such as limited reach, mobility, hearing, or vision, to learn about his or her special housing needs. (The disability can be temporary, such as a broken leg, or permanent.) Briefly describe the person in the space below, then answer the following questions.

Description of the person:

_____

_____

_____

_____

_____

1. What qualities about this person affect his or her housing needs?

_____

_____

_____

_____

_____

_____

2. In what ways are this person's special housing needs being met?

_____

_____

_____

_____

_____

_____

3. Which special housing needs are *not* being met? Why?

_____

_____

_____

_____

_____

_____

Places to Live

Name _____

Date _____ Period _____

omplete the following sentences by placing the missing word(s) in the preceding blanks.

_____ 1. The specific part of the world, country, or state in which you live is your _____.

_____ 2. A large city, a rural area, or a small village would be an example of a _____.

_____ 3. A(n) _____ neighborhood is occupied by living units.

_____ 4. Stores and businesses are commonly found in a _____ neighborhood.

_____ 5. _____ neighborhoods include businesses, factories, warehouses, and industrial plants.

_____ 6. Some neighborhoods have _____ rules which require that the land and buildings be used for only one purpose.

_____ 7. _____ are a set of limits or rules that may be made by housing developers to assure that all owners will maintain a certain style of living.

_____ 8. A(n) _____ neighborhood is usually in a zoned area where restrictions determine the size and layout of individual lots before anything is built.

_____ 9. In a(n) _____ neighborhood, the residents' age, ethnic background, income level, or occupation usually vary.

_____ 10. People of similar backgrounds reside in a _____ neighborhood.

_____ 11. A(n) _____ is the piece of land on which the dwelling is built.

_____ 12. A natural restraint of a site is the _____, which refers to the slope or lay of the land.

_____ 13. Adding decorative plantings to an area is a method of _____ used to change the appearance of the site.

_____ 14. _____ to sun and wind affect the level of comfort within various rooms of a home.

_____ 15. _____ _____ _____ (MPS), set by the Federal Housing Administration, regulate the sizes of lots.

_____ 16. The _____ zone is the part of a site that can be seen from the street.

_____ 17. The _____ zone is the part of the site that is used for necessary activities.

_____ 18. The _____ zone, used for recreation and relaxation, can be separated from the public zone by using shrubs, hedges, screens, fences, or walls.

_____ 19. A(n) _____ house is a type of dwelling designed for more than one living unit.

_____ 20. Multifamily _____ range from tenement quarters to exclusive penthouses.

(Continued)

_____21. When people move into a _____-_____, they "buy" their apartment by pur chasing shares in a nonprofit corporation that owns the building.

_____22. _____ owners purchase a dwelling in the same way they would purchase detached house, but share the ownership of the lot, parking areas, recreationa facilities, and hallways.

_____23. The most desired type of housing is the _____-_____ house.

_____24. Townhouses and row houses are types of _____ houses.

_____25. A(n) _____ _____ is a type of single-family house that shares a common wall wit another house.

_____26. A(n) _____-_____ and custom-built house is the most individualistic type c house. Often called a dream house, it is built by a contractor according to a architect's plans and the purchasers' wishes.

_____27. When a house is _____-_____ from stock plans, the owners choose a house plan an have a contractor build the house for them on their site.

_____28. People with considerable skill, time, and energy, may choose an _____-___ house.

_____29. A(n) _____ house is built by a developer who builds an entire neighborhood a once.

_____30. _____-_____ housing is constructed in a plant and moved to a site.

_____31. A(n) _____ house is built as a shell in the factory and later completed at the sit according to the buyer's wishes.

_____32. _____ housing is factory-built in a coordinated series of modules.

_____33. A design approach that makes houses easier for everyone to use is _____ ____

_____34. The _____ _____ _____ forbids discrimination in housing and requires multiunit to be accessible to people with disabilities.

_____35. The _____ _____ _____ is a receipt listing the items shipped by a professiona moving company.

Acquiring Housing

A Place to Rent

Activity A

Chapter 5

Name _____

Date _____ Period _____

Make an appointment to see or visit an apartment that is open to the public and fill out the Apartment Renters' Checklist. Interview the landlord and record his or her comments using the Questions for the Landlord that follow. Then summarize your thoughts about the apartment in the Apartment Evaluation.

Apartment Renters' Checklist

Laundry facilities

_____ How many washers and dryers are available? (A good ratio is one washer and dryer for every ten apartments)

_____ Are washers and dryers in good working order?

Building lobby

_____ Is the lobby clean and well lit?

_____ Is the main entrance locked so only residents can enter?

_____ Is a security guard provided? If so, what hours?

Entrance, exit, and halls

_____ Are elevators provided? If so, are they in good working order?

_____ Are the stairs soundly constructed and well lit?

_____ Are fire exits provided?

_____ Is there a fire alarm or other warning system?

_____ Are halls clean, well lit, and soundly constructed?

Bathroom(s)

_____ Do all plumbing fixtures work? Are they clean?

_____ Does the hot water supply seem adequate?

_____ Do floors and walls around fixtures seem damp, rotted, or moldy?

Kitchen

_____ Is the sink working and clean? Does it have drain stoppers?

_____ Is there an exhaust fan above the range?

_____ Is the refrigerator working properly? Does it have a separate freezer compartment?

_____ If there is a dishwasher, does it work properly?

Air conditioning

_____ Is the building centrally air conditioned or are separate units present for each apartment?

_____ Does the air conditioning unit work properly?

Heating

_____ What type of heat is provided (gas, electric)?

_____ Does the heating system work properly?

_____ Is there a fireplace? If so, are there smoke stains or any other signs that it has not worked properly?

(Continued)

Wiring

_____ Are there enough electrical outlets? (There should be at least three to a room.)
_____ Do all switches and outlets work?
_____ Are there enough circuits in the fuse box or circuit breaker panel to handle all your electrical equipment?

Lighting

_____ Are there enough fixtures for adequate light? Are the fixtures in good working order?
_____ Does the apartment get a good amount of natural light from windows?

Windows

_____ Are any windows broken or difficult to open and close?
_____ Are windows arranged to provide good ventilation?
_____ Are screens provided?
_____ Are there drafts around the window frame?
_____ In high-rise buildings, does the landlord arrange for the outside of the windows to be cleaned? If so, how often?

Floors

_____ Are floors clean and free of gouges?
_____ Do floors have any water stains indicating previous leaks?

Ceilings

_____ Are ceilings clean and free of cracks and peeling?
_____ Are there any water stains indicating previous leaks?

Walls

_____ Are walls clean and free of cracks and peeling?
_____ Does the paint run or smear when rubbed with a damp cloth?

Soundproofing

_____ When you thump the walls, do they seem hollow or solid?
_____ Can you hear neighbors downstairs, upstairs, or on either side of you?

Telephone

_____ Are phone jacks already installed?
_____ Are phone jacks in convenient locations?

Television

_____ Is an outside antenna connection provided?
_____ Is a cable TV connection provided?

Storage space

_____ Is there adequate closet space?
_____ Are there enough kitchen and bathroom cabinets?
_____ Is additional storage space provided tor tenants?

Outdoor play space

_____ Are outdoor facilities provided? If so, are the facilities well maintained?

(Continued)

Questions for the Landlord

1. What is the rent per month? How and when must it be paid? _____

_____

_____

2. Is a security deposit required? If so, how much is it? Under what conditions will it be returned?

_____

_____

_____

_____

3. Does the lease say that rent can be increased if real estate or other expenses to the landlord are
raised? _____

_____

4. What expenses are there in addition to rent? (These may include utilities, storage space, air conditioning, parking space, master TV antenna connections, use of a pool or other recreational areas,
installation of special appliances, and late payment of rent.)_____

_____

_____

_____

_____

5. How are deliveries of packages handled? _____

_____

_____

6. Is loud noise prohibited at certain hours? _____

Apartment Evaluation

Describe your overall impression of this apartment.

_____

_____

_____

_____

Based on your completed evaluation, would you like to live in this apartment? Why?

_____

_____

_____

_____

_____

_____

The Written Lease

Name _____

Date _____ Period _____

Imagine that you have signed the lease shown as Figure 5-5 in the text. Review the lease for answers to the following questions.

1. According to the lease, what might happen if you damage the landlord's property? _____

   _____

   _____

   _____

2. What is the landlord required to provide if your security deposit is withheld because of damage to the apartment? _____

   _____

   _____

   _____

3. You decide to move when your lease expires. In what condition must you leave the apartment when you move? _____

   _____

   _____

4. The roof leaks and damages your television. Is the landlord responsible for the damage to your television? _____

   _____

5. You find that paying the rent and other expenses are more difficult than you had expected. Can you get a roommate to move in and share expenses with you? _____

   _____

6. Can you paint and paper the walls? _____

   _____

7. Can you install partitions in your living room? _____

   _____

8. Can you install new locks on the doors? _____

   _____

9. Can you place campaign signs in your windows? _____

   _____

10. Are you allowed to have a waterbed? _____

    _____

11. Can you give piano lessons in your apartment? _____

    _____

(Continued)

2. Are you allowed to have a barbecue on the balcony? _____
   _____

3. Are you allowed to keep a dog? _____
   _____

4. When and under what circumstances must you allow your landlord free access to your apartment?
   _____
   _____
   _____
   _____
   _____

5. Your bicycle is stolen from the storage room. Is your landlord liable? _____

6. Under the terms of the lease, what are the possible consequences if you move out before the lease expires? _____
   _____
   _____

7. Under the terms of the lease, what are the possible consequences if you fail to pay your rent?
   _____
   _____
   _____
   _____
   _____

8. Under the terms of the lease, what are the possible consequences if you fail to comply with the terms of the lease? _____
   _____
   _____
   _____
   _____
   _____

Buying or Renting

Activity C   Name _____

Chapter 5   Date _____ Period _____

Look through the classified section of the newspaper and find two ads for available houses: on "for sale" and one "for rent." Clip and mount the examples in the spaces provided. List the advantage and disadvantages of each.

"For Sale" House Ad

Advantages: _____   Disadvantages: _____

_____   _____

_____   _____

_____   _____

"For Rent" House Ad

Advantages: _____   Disadvantages: _____

_____   _____

_____   _____

_____   _____

Would you rather buy or rent a house? Why?

_____

_____

_____

_____

_____

Real Estate

Name _____

Date _____ Period _____

Record the information presented by the guest real estate agent on the availability of housing in your community.

Name of real estate agent: _____ Company represented: _____

List the responsibilities of a real estate agent.

_____

_____

_____

_____

When should someone seek the services of a real estate agent?

_____

_____

_____

_____

List types of real estate available in your community.

_____

_____

_____

_____

Describe the procedure to follow when contacting a real estate agent about buying or renting a house.

_____

_____

_____

_____

Once a buyer has found a house, how long does it usually take to settle legal and financial matters so the buyer can move in? _____

_____

Additional noteworthy facts:

_____

_____

_____

_____

_____

_____

Buying a House

Name_____

Date_____ Period _____

Estimate your likely income in 10 years and the price of a house you can buy. Then mount a picture of housing that is available now at that price.

1. Estimate your annual gross income.

    •Expected employment (type of job):_____

    •Likely annual gross income (based on current salary statistics): $ _____

    •Likely annual gross income of spouse (if a marriage is not
        anticipated, enter zero.): $ _____

    •Total family annual gross income: $ _____

2. Multiply the total family annual gross income x 2½.

    •Estimated price of an affordable house: $ _____

3. From a newspaper or real estate brochure, find a house, condominium, or co-op that will fit into your housing budget. Mount a picture of it in the space below.

Selling price of the home: $_____

The Details of Acquiring Housing

Activity F   Name _____

Chapter 5   Date _____ Period _____

Complete the following sentences by placing the missing word(s) in the preceding blanks.

_____ 1. _____ in housing refers to the method you use to acquire any part of your housing.

_____ 2. Securing a purchase by paying part of the total now involves a _____ _____.

_____ 3. _____ buying involves making a down payment and paying the balance over a period of months or years.

_____ 4. In addition to the spending of money, _____ also means the spending of other resources.

_____ 5. A(n) _____ _____ is a fee paid for the privilege of using credit.

_____ 6. _____ is the price paid for the use of money.

_____ 7. _____ charges are the amounts other than interest that are added to the price of something when it is bought in installments.

_____ 8. Over one-third of all Americans _____ their homes.

_____ 9. The owner of rental property is called a _____ or landlord.

_____ 10. A(n) _____ deposit insures the landlord against financial loss in case the renter fails to pay the rent or damages the dwelling.

_____ 11. A(n) _____ _____ is a legal document spelling out the conditions under which the tenant rents the property.

_____ 12. To _____ a lease, you transfer the entire unused portion of the lease to someone else.

_____ 13. To _____ a lease, you transfer part interest in the property to someone else.

_____ 14. _____ _____ _____ is the legal term used for failure to meet all terms of a contract or agreement.

_____ 15. The process of forcing a renter to leave the property before the rental agreement expires is called _____.

_____ 16. The dollar value of your house beyond what is owed on the house is called _____.

_____ 17. Your total income before deductions are made is called _____ income.

_____ 18. _____ is the legal proceeding in which a lending firm takes possession of the property.

(Continued)

_____19. Contractors who want to build a house should submit a _____ to the buyer telling how much will be charged for constructing the house.

_____20. A(n) _____ will judge the construction and present condition of a house.

_____21. A(n) _____ will give you an expert estimate of the quality and value of the property.

_____22. An agreement of sale should include the amount of the _____ _____, or cash paid by the buyer toward the cost of the house.

_____23. A(n) _____ of title is a copy of all public records concerning a piece of property.

_____24. Before funding a loan, a lender may have a _____ done to be sure that a building is actually sited on the land according to the legal description.

_____25. A home buyer may purchase title _____ for protection against financial loss caused by errors in the abstract of title.

_____26. A(n) _____ is a pledge of property that a borrower gives to a lender as security for the payment of a debt.

_____27. The _____-_____ mortgage is a three-party contract involving the borrower, lending firm, and the Federal Housing Administration.

_____28. A _____-_____ mortgage is less-costly, fixed-rate loan, available only to veterans of the U.S. Armed Forces.

_____29. The fees and amounts charged for settling legal and financial matters before the sale of real estate is final are called _____ costs.

_____30. The _____ is a document that gives proof of the rights of ownership and possession of a specific property.

_____31. The _____ describes the property being sold and is signed and witnessed according to the laws of the state where the property is located.

_____32. People may choose to _____ a mortgage to lower monthly payments.

_____33. The _____ _____ _____ contains the conditions and restrictions of the sale, ownership, and use of the property within a particular group of condominium units.

_____34. A(n) fee is a monthly payment from condominium owners for the repair and upkeep of the common areas.

The Evolution of Exteriors

Roof and Dwelling Styles

Activity A   Name _____

Chapter 6   Date _____ Period _____

Label these roof and dwelling styles.

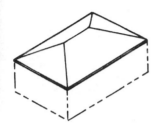

1. _____

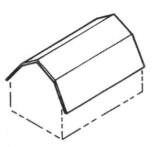

2. _____

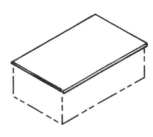

3. _____

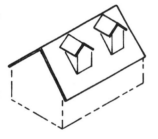

4. _____

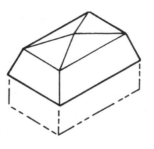

5. _____

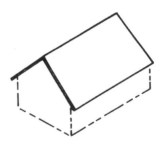

6. _____

7. _____

8. _____

9. _____

10. _____

11. _____

12. _____

Origin and Style

Name_____

Date_____ Period _____

Read each of the descriptions below. Fill in the origin of the house it describes in the left column. Fill the housing style to which it refers in the right column.

Origin	Description	Housing Style
1. _____	These eight-sided structures are usually made of logs and mud. The door always faces east as a matter of religious belief.	_____
2. _____	These dwellings have a flat roof, boxy construction, and projecting beams. They are arranged in an apartment-type community.	_____
3. _____	These asymmetrically designed dwellings contain characteristics such as a red tile roof, an enclosed patio, arch-shaped windows and doors, wrought iron exterior decor, and stucco walls. They are mainly used where the climate is warm and dry.	_____
4. _____	This one-story rectangular building contains a few windows and a gable roof. It is built of unfinished logs.	_____
5. _____	These houses have a gambrel roof with eaves that flare outward. Other characteristics include a central entrance, a chimney that is not centered, dormers in the second story, and windows with small panes. The houses are usually built of fieldstone or brick.	_____
6. _____	The roof of this house is a variation of the gambrel roof. The roof is steeply pitched and may contain dormers.	_____
7. _____	This house has a delicate, dignified appearance and is usually symmetrical. The tops of the windows break into the eave line.	_____
8. _____	This small, symmetrical, one-and-one-half story house has a gable roof. It also has a central entrance and a central chimney with several fireplaces.	_____

(Continued

Origin	Description	Housing Style
9. _____	This house is based on the basic Cape Cod design modified with a lean-to section added to the back. It is usually two or two-and-one-half stories high with a steep gable roof that extends down to the first floor in the rear.	_____
0. _____	Named after forts, these structures have an overhanging second story which allows additional space on the second floor. The overhang also provides extra support for the second story floor. The designs are symmetrical with steep gable roofs and windows with small panes of glass.	_____
1. _____	Adapted during the era when England was ruled by Kings George I, II, and III, these houses have simple, symmetrical exterior lines with either a hip or gable roof style. They have tall chimneys at each end of the roof.	_____
2. _____	This symmetrical house is at least two stories high with a boxlike shape. It has a flat roof surrounded by a balustrade and pediments over the porticoes, doors, or windows.	_____
3. _____	A house of this style is large and impressive. The main characteristic is a two-story portico supported by columns. It also has a large triangular pediment.	_____
4. _____	An offshoot of the Greek Revival style, this two-story house has columns that extend across the front covered by an extension of the roof. The house is large and symmetrical with a hip or gable roof.	_____
5. _____	Named after the Queen of England, this house style contains an abundance of decorative trim with high porches, steep gable roofs, tall windows, and a turret or small tower. The inside features high ceilings and long halls.	_____

Housing Styles

Name_____

Date_____ Period _____

Describe these housing styles in your own words.

Traditional: _____

_____

_____

Modern:_____

_____

_____

Contemporary:_____

_____

_____

Look through magazines or the housing section of the newspaper. Clip and mount picture representing each of these styles. Show and discuss these housing styles in class.

Traditional

(Continue

Modern

Contemporary

Your Choice of Exteriors

Name _____

Date _____ Period _____

Express your opinions about your likes and dislikes regarding the exterior styles in house designs presented in Chapter 6.

Designs I like: _____

_____

Reasons: _____

_____

_____

_____

_____

Designs I dislike: _____

_____

Reasons: _____

_____

_____

_____

_____

Design choices available in the community: _____

_____

_____

_____

_____

_____

Design(s) I want in my future home (explain): _____

_____

_____

_____

_____

_____

_____

_____

_____

_____

_____

Evolution of Exteriors Word Puzzle

Activity E

Chapter 6

Name _____

Date _____ Period _____

ill in the word puzzle with terms and concepts from the chapter. See the clues on the next page.

1											E											
2											V											
3											O											
4											L											
5											U											
6											T											
7											I											
8											O											
9											N											
10											O											
11											F											
12											E											
13											X											
14											T											
15											E											
16											R											
17											I											
18											O											
19											R											
20											S											

(Continued)

1. The Pueblo in New Mexico live in _____ houses.

2. The symmetrical _____ _____ house may be two-and-one-half stories high.

3. The Swedish and Finnish immigrants brought the _____ _____ to North America.

4. The main features of the _____ _____ style is a two-story portico supported by Greek columns with a large triangular pediment.

5. The _____ _____ style was first built in New York and Delaware.

6. Good designs created in the past that have survived the test of time are called _____ styles.

7. The _____ style of house has an overhanging second story like the old forts.

8. Some styles designed by English architects are named for _____ _____.

9. House styles developed in the recent past are known as _____.

10. The Federal style sometimes has a(n) _____.

11. The _____ style developed following the American Revolution.

12. A(n) _____ is a small tower on a Victorian house.

13. The _____ house, with its lean-to section, is a variation of the Cape Cod style.

14. Haunted houses in horror movies are usually in _____ style.

15. The _____ house has porches and terraces that expand the living space.

16. _____ houses cover large areas and are expensive to build.

17. The architect who designed the prairie house was _____ _____ _____.

18. House styles that are of the latest designs and are surprising and often controversial are called _____.

19. Energy from the sun is used to heat _____ houses.

20. Active and passive solar power is found in many _____-_____ houses.

....

Understanding House Plans

Floor Plan Symbols

Activity A

Chapter 7

Name _____

Date _____ Period _____

Identify these symbols, which are often used in floor plans.

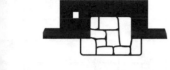

1. _____

7. _____

13. _____

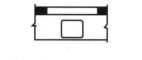

2. _____

8. _____

14. _____

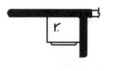

3. _____

9. _____

15. _____

4. _____

10. _____

16. _____

5. _____

11. _____

17. _____

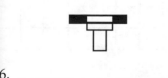

6. _____

12. _____

18. _____

Drawing a Room to Scale

Activity B

Chapter 7

Name _____

Date _____ Period _____

Draw your classroom to scale on the graph paper below. Apply the appropriate symbols where needed.

Scale: ¼ inch = 1 foot

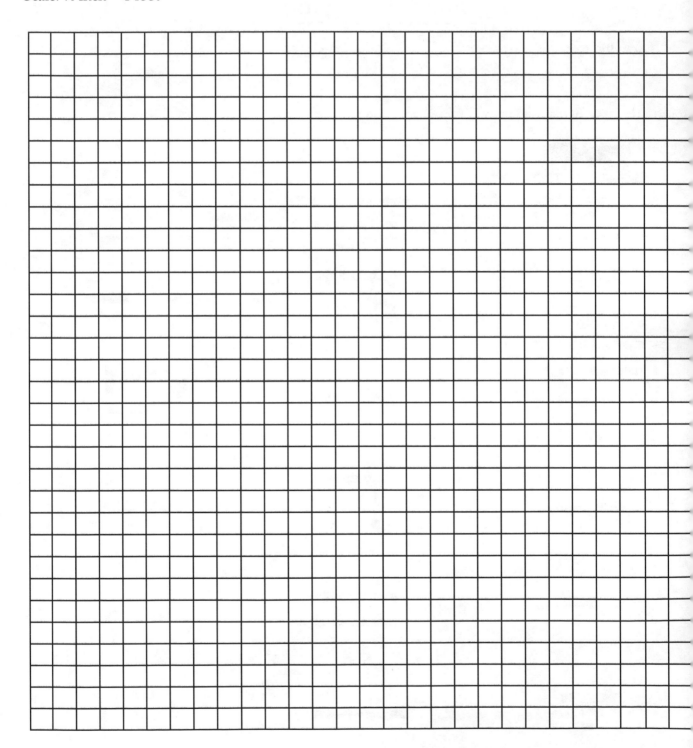

Clothing Storage

Name_____

Date_____ Period _____

Determine the storage need. Then sketch ways of improving the storage space in this traditional closet. Use the space below to describe your changes.

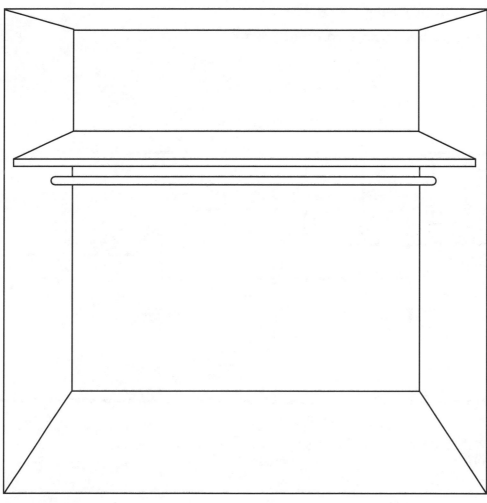

Description of changes:

_____

_____

_____

_____

_____

_____

_____

_____

_____

Floor Plan Evaluation

Activity D

Chapter 7

Name _____

Date _____ Period _____

Complete the following steps using the floor plan below.

1. Shade in the quiet area using a blue pencil.
2. Shade in the work area using a yellow pencil.
3. Shade in the social area using a red pencil.
4. Shade in the built-in storage area using an orange pencil.
5. Indicate traffic patterns with lines using a green pencil.

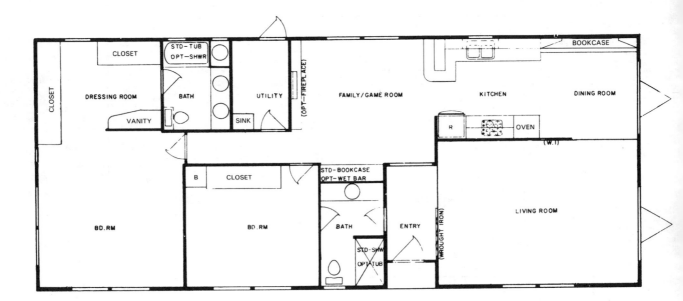

Describe the family members (number, ages, special needs, activities, etc.) who might live in the hous
shown on this floor plan.

_____

_____

_____

_____

_____

_____

_____

_____

_____

_____

(Continued

On the basis of the description of this family, evaluate the floor plan according to the following:

1. Quiet area: _____
_____
_____
_____
_____
_____
_____

2. Work area: _____
_____
_____
_____
_____
_____
_____
_____

3. Social area: _____
_____
_____
_____
_____
_____
_____
_____

4. Built-in storage area: _____
_____
_____
_____
_____
_____
_____

5. Traffic patterns: _____
_____
_____
_____
_____
_____
_____

Understanding Plans for a House

Activity E

Chapter 7

Name _____

Date _____ Period _____

Complete the following sentences by placing the missing word(s) in the preceding blanks.

_____ 1. _____ _____ contain information about the size, shape, and location of all part of a house.

_____ 2. Types and quality of materials to be used and directions for their use are stated in the _____.

_____ 3. A copy of an architectural drawing is called a _____.

_____ 4. Seven different types of lines commonly used on architectural drawings are called the _____ _____ _____.

_____ 5. _____ lines show alternate positions, repeated details, and paths of motion.

_____ 6. _____ lines show the outline of the building and walls.

_____ 7. _____ lines show edges of surfaces that are not visible in a specific view of a house.

_____ 8. _____ lines show the center of an arc or circle.

_____ 9. _____ lines show the size and location of a dimension.

_____ 10. _____ lines show the termination points of a dimension.

_____ 11. _____ lines show that an object continues on, but the complete view is not shown.

_____ 12. _____ lines are often called crosshatch lines.

_____ 13. Plumbing and electrical fixtures, doors, windows, and other common objects in a house are represented by _____.

_____ 14. Views of a house taken from the top of an imaginary glass box are called _____ _____

_____ 15. A simplified drawing that shows the size and arrangement of rooms, hallways, doors, windows, and storage areas on one floor of a house is called a _____ _____

_____ 16. Architectural drawings that show the outside views of a house are called _____ _____.

_____ 17. A(n) _____ _____ shows the finished exterior appearance of a given side of a house.

_____ 18. A view taken from an imaginary cut through a part of a house, such as the walls, is called a _____ _____.

_____ 19. A(n) enlargement of a construction feature is often shown in a _____ _____.

_____ 20. The _____ area in most houses consists of bedrooms and bathrooms.

_____ 21. Bedrooms that provide space for activities such as reading, studying, watching TV, listening to music, and working on hobbies are called _____ rooms.

_____ 22. All areas of a house that are needed to maintain and service the other areas are called the _____ area.

_____ 23. The three activity centers in the kitchen are connected by an imaginary _____ _____

House Construction

Construction Materials

Activity A   Name_____

Chapter 8   Date_____ Period _____

Complete the following chart by identifying the advantages and disadvantages of various construction materials.

Construction Material	Advantages	Disadvantages
Wood siding types:		
Manufactured siding types:		
Masonry siding types:		
Roofing shingles types:		
Tile, slate, and concrete roofing materials:		
Metal roofing types:		

Foundation and Framing

Name _____

Date _____ Period _____

Briefly describe each term listed below. Then label the indicated parts of the house illustrated on the next page with the corresponding letters.

A. Floor girder _____

_____

B. Floor joist _____

_____

C. Footing _____

_____

D. Foundation wall _____

_____

E. Header _____

_____

F. Rafter _____

_____

G. Ridge _____

_____

H. Sill plate _____

_____

I. Stud _____

_____

J. Subflooring _____

(Continued)

1.
2.
3.
4.
5.
6.
7.
8.
9.
10.

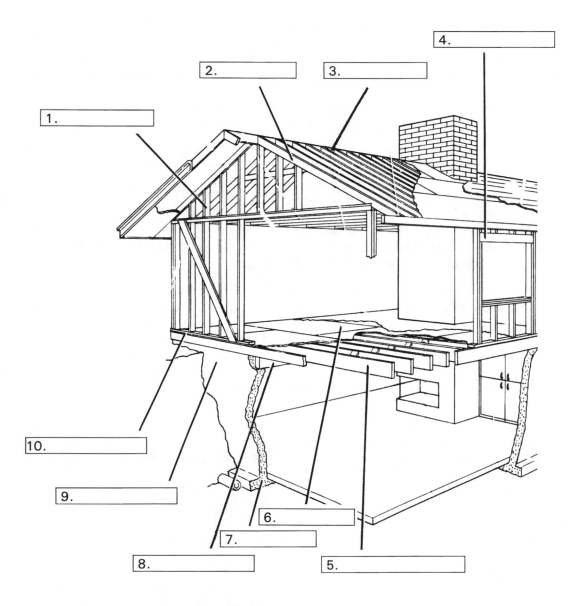

Choosing Windows and Doors

Activity C

Chapter 8

Name _____

Date _____ Period _____

The Adams family needs to make some decisions about windows and doors in their home. Read about their housing goals and answer the questions to help them meet their needs.

1. What are three functions that everyone wants a window to provide? _____
   _____

2. To keep fuel bills down, what energy-efficient materials might the family select for the windows?
   _____

3. The family wants the front of the house to have a contemporary look. What type of windows might create this appearance? _____

4. Mr. Adams wants plenty of ventilation in the kitchen. What type of windows might he select for the room? _____

5. Mr. and Mrs. Adams want fresh air in the children's playroom in the basement. However, the children do not always remember to close windows before leaving a room. This caused several pieces of playroom furniture to be damaged during a recent rainstorm. What type of window might be a good choice to prevent this from happening again? _____

6. Mrs. Adams wants to clean windows and screens in the upstairs bedrooms without standing on a ladder outside the house. What type of windows might she select for these rooms? _____
   _____

7. The dining room is air conditioned, so windows are not needed for ventilation. However, there is a lovely view outside the dining room window. The family wants the window to serve as a focal point in the room. What type of window might they select for this room? _____
   _____

8. The family room is located in the center of the house. Because there are no windows, the room seems rather dark. What can the family do to give the room a brighter, more airy appearance? _____
   _____

9. Mrs. Adams wants to install a door between the kitchen and the dining room. However, the refrigerator is located on one side of the doorway, and cabinets are mounted on the other side. This leaves little room for a door to swing open and close. What type of door might she choose for this location? _____
   _____

10. Mr. Adams wants the front door to provide security and serve as a weather barrier. What type of door might he choose for the front of the house? _____
    _____

11. The family room doubles as a guest room when the Adams family has visitors. The family wants to install a lightweight door at the entrance to the family room to provide privacy. What type of door might they install? _____

12. Outside the living room is a patio and a flower garden. The family wants this outside area to be visible and accessible from the living room. What type of door might they install to achieve this goal?
    _____

. . . .

The Systems Within

Electricity in Your Home

Activity A   Name _____

Chapter 9   Date _____ Period _____

n the following lines, list 20 items in your home that are powered by electricity. Then answer the
uestion below.

_____   _____

_____   _____

_____   _____

_____   _____

_____   _____

_____   _____

_____   _____

_____   _____

_____   _____

_____   _____

ow would your life be different without electrical power in your home? (Use complete sentences to
rite a fairly detailed response.)

_____

_____

_____

_____

_____

_____

_____

_____

_____

_____

_____

Household Plumbing

Name _____

Date _____ Period _____

Find magazine or catalog pictures showing bathroom fixtures that you would select for your home. Mount the pictures in the space below, then answer the questions that follow.

1. Which of the fixtures pictured require a hot water branch line? _____

_____

2. Where does the hot water main start in a house? _____

3. Why are shutoff valves installed on each branch line next to each fixture or appliance? _____

_____

4. How do waste disposal pipes differ from water supply lines? _____

_____

5. How are gases from the wastewater removal system removed? _____

_____

6. What is the purpose of a trap in a plumbing fixture? _____

_____

_____

Heating Systems

Name _____

Date _____ Period _____

Complete the information below to describe three different heating systems. Then decide which of these systems you would choose for your home and explain your choice.

1. Heating system: _____

   Fuel used: _____

   How is the air heated and circulated? _____

   _____

   _____

   Advantages: _____

   _____

   Disadvantages: _____

   _____

2. Heating system: _____

   Fuel used: _____

   How is the air heated and circulated? _____

   _____

   _____

   Advantages: _____

   _____

   Disadvantages: _____

   _____

3. Heating system: _____

   Fuel used: _____

   How is the air heated and circulated? _____

   _____

   _____

   Advantages: _____

   _____

   Disadvantages: _____

My choice of heating system is _____

My reasons for choosing this system are _____

_____

_____

Systems Savvy

Name _____

Date _____ Period _____

Match the following terms and identifying phrases.

_____ 1. The movement of electrons along a conductor.

_____ 2. The path followed by electrons from a source of electricity to a device and back to the source.

_____ 3. A vertical pipe that extends through the roof so gases from the wastewater removal system may vent outside.

_____ 4. A circulating hot water system.

_____ 5. A measurement of electrical power.

_____ 6. A device that monitors electrical usage in the home.

_____ 7. A measure of the pressure used to push electrical current along a conductor.

_____ 8. The unit of current used to measure the amount of electricity passing through a conductor per unit of time.

_____ 9. The resistance of a material to heat movement.

_____ 10. A metal or plastic pipe that surrounds and protects wires.

_____ 11. A material used to restrict the flow of heat from out of a home in winter and into the home in summer.

_____ 12. Something—usually a wire—that allows a flow of electricity.

_____ 13. A system that uses resistance wiring to produce heat in wire.

_____ 14. A large metal box that receives power from an electric company's service drop or service lateral.

_____ 15. A strip of material that covers the edges of a window or door to prevent moisture and air from entering a home.

_____ 16. The connecting wires from a pole transformer to the point of entry to a home.

_____ 17. A device that catches and holds a quantity of water in a plumbing fixture in order to prevent sewage gases from coming back into a home.

_____ 18. An electric refrigeration unit used to either heat or cool a home.

_____ 19. Fuses or circuit breakers used to stop an excessive flow of electrical current in a circuit if too much current is being drawn.

_____ 20. A system in which air is heated by a furnace and then delivered to rooms through supply ducts.

A. ampere
B. central heat-pump system
C. circuit
D. conductor
E. conduit
F. electric current
G. electricity
H. electric radiant-heating system
I. fireplace insert
J. forced warm-air system
K. hydropic heating system
L. insulation
M. meter
N. overcurrent protection devices
O. R-value
P. service drop
Q. service entrance panel
R. soil stack
S. trap
T. voltage
U. watt
V. weather stripping

. . . .

Elements of Design

Design Characteristics

Activity A   Name _____

Chapter 10   Date _____ Period _____

reate a new product. Carefully consider the function, construction, and aesthetics of your design. In
ie space below, sketch your product. Then answer the questions that follow.

1. What is your product called? _____

2. What will your product do or how will it be used? _____

_____

3. To what ages, sizes, and ability levels does this product appeal? _____

_____

_____

4. From what materials will your product be made? _____

_____

5. Why did you choose these particular materials to construct your product? _____

_____

_____

6. Why do you think your potential customers will be pleased with this product?_____

_____

_____

Lines

Name_____

Date_____ Period _____

Connect the dots in Part 1 and identify the lines that result. Provide the information requested in Part 2

Part 1

A •

A •   B •   B •

1. _____   2. _____

A •

A •   B •

A •   C •

B •   D •

F •   E •

3. _____   4. _____

Part 2

5. Define *line*:_____

_____

Different types of lines create different emotional responses. Indicate the feeling or emotions produced by each of the following lines:

6. Horizontal—_____

7. Vertical—_____

8. Diagonal—_____

9. Curved—_____

10. List three ways to use lines in housing decisions.

_____

_____

_____

_____

_____

Form

Name_____

Date_____ Period _____

In each square below, draw an example or mount a clipping showing the type of form indicated. Then follow the directions.

Realistic   Abstract

Geometric   Free Form

List the three guidelines for using form in design. Give an example of each guideline.

Guidelines   Examples

1. _____   _____

   _____   _____

2. _____   _____

   _____   _____

3. _____   _____

   _____   _____

Space and Mass

Activity D

Chapter 10

Name _____

Date _____ Period _____

Answer the following questions about space and mass as elements of design.

1. Define *space*. _____

_____

2. What is the size of the space in your bedroom?

Height: _____ Length: _____ Width: _____

3. Who uses this space? _____

_____

4. How is this space used? _____

_____

5. What feelings are created by this space? _____

_____

6. How can you use space in housing to create a feeling of grandeur? _____

_____

7. How can you use space in housing to create a cozy feeling? _____

_____

8. Define *mass*. _____

_____

9. How are space and mass related to form? _____

_____

10. In the spaces below, mount or draw pictures illustrating the types of mass indicated.

High Mass   **Low Mass**

Using Color Effectively

Psychological Effects of Color

Activity A

Chapter 11

Name _____

Date _____ Period _____

Describe how each color listed below makes you feel. Then answer the questions that follow. Compare your responses with those of others in the class.

Red: _____

_____

Orange: _____

_____

Yellow: _____

_____

Green: _____

_____

Blue: _____

_____

Violet: _____

_____

Black: _____

_____

White: _____

_____

Considering your responses to each of these colors, which would you choose as the main color for your bedroom? Why? _____

_____

_____

Which color would you prefer for a game room? Why? _____

_____

_____

Which color would you like least for a dining room? Why? _____

_____

_____

The Color Wheel

Name_____

Date_____ Period _____

Complete the following statements by writing the correct terms in the blanks. Then color in the color wheel below.

1. By mixing, lightening, and darkening the _____ colors, all other colors can be made.

2. Mixing equal amounts of any two primary colors produces a(n) _____ color.

3. The _____ colors are named after the two colors used to make them, with the primary color listed first.

4. Red-orange, yellow-orange, yellow-green, blue-green, blue-violet, and red-violet are _____ colors.

5. Red, yellow, and blue are the _____ colors.

6. Green, orange, and violet are _____ colors.

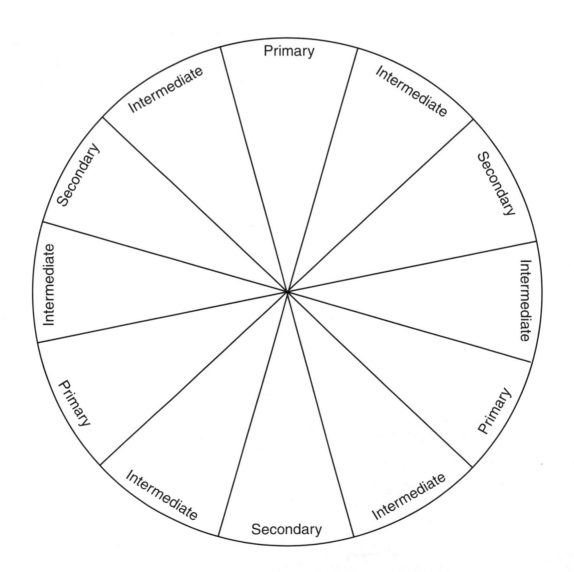

Tints and Shades

Name _____

Date _____ Period _____

Look at the value scale in Figure 11-4 of the text. Create value scales below with values ranging from tints to shades with two colors from the color wheel.

Color 1 **Color 2**

Tints

Color:

Shades

Color Quiz

Name _____

Date _____ Period _____

Complete the following sentences by placing the missing word(s) in the preceding blanks.

_____ 1.   The _____ _____ forms the basis of all color relationships.

_____ 2.   A(n) _____ is the name of a color.

_____ 3.   The lightness or darkness of a color is called its _____.

_____ 4.   A(n) _____ results when white is added to a color to produce a lighter value.

_____ 5.   A(n) _____ results when black is added to a color to produce a darker value.

_____ 6.   The brightness or dullness of a hue is its _____.

_____ 7.   The _____ of a hue is the hue positioned directly opposite it on a color wheel.

_____ 8.   Black, white, and gray are _____.

_____ 9.   Advancing colors such as red and orange are often called _____ colors.

_____ 10. Receding colors such as blue and green are often called _____ colors.

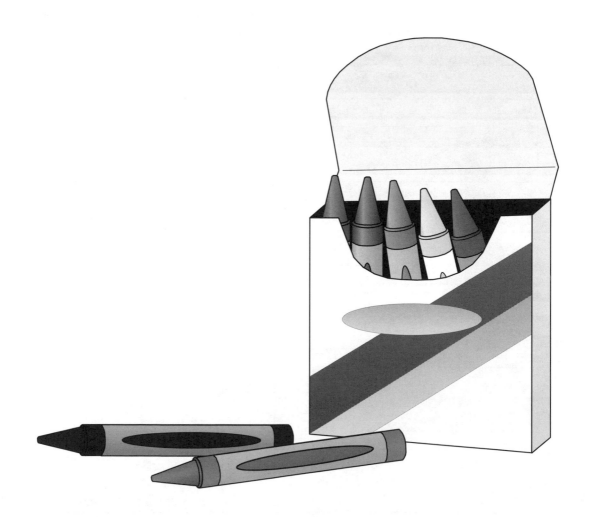

Color Harmonies

Activity E

Chapter 11

Name_____

Date_____ Period _____

Match one color harmony and one color combination to each of the following descriptions. Write the appropriate letters in the spaces provided. Then use the chart below to describe two different color harmonies and show examples with pictures or fabric swatches.

Harmony	Colors	Description:
_____ – _____		1. The simplest color harmony in which variation is added by changing the value and intensity of a single hue.
_____ – _____		2. A color harmony made by combining related hues that are next to each other on the color wheel.
_____ – _____		3. A color harmony using colors located opposite each other on the color wheel.
_____ – _____		4. A color harmony which uses a main color and the colors on both sides of its complement.
_____ – _____		5. A color harmony which does not use the two basic complementary colors, but the two pairs of colors to the sides of the complements instead.
_____ – _____		6. A color harmony which uses three colors that are spaced evenly around the color wheel.

Harmonies

A. Analogous
B. Split complementary
C. Monochromatic
D. Triad
E. Complementary
F. Double complementary

Color Combinations

G. Red, orange, green, blue
H. Orange, blue
I. Light blue, medium blue, dark blue
J. Red-violet, yellow-orange, blue-green
K. Yellow, yellow-green, green
L. Violet, yellow-orange, yellow-green

Color Harmony 1	Color Harmony 2
Name of color harmony: _____ Colors used: _____	Name of color harmony: _____ Colors used: _____

Designing with Color

Name _____

Date _____ Period _____

Pretend that you are redecorating a room in your home. Answer the following questions to help you decide what color harmony to use.

1. What room will you be redecorating? _____

2. What type of mood do you want to create in this room? _____

3. What type of style do you want to create in this room? _____

4. Who uses this room? How will the lifestyles of these people affect your choice of colors? _____

   _____

   _____

5. What activities occur in this room? _____

   _____

6. What furniture and accessories will be used in this room? Specify the main colors in each item.

   _____

   _____

7. What type of lighting is used in this room? _____

8. What direction does this room face? _____

9. What rooms adjoin this room? Specify the base color in each room. _____

   _____

   _____

10. What size is this room?

    Length: _____ Width: _____ Height: _____

11. What color harmony do you plan to use in this room? _____

12. What will you use as your base color? _____

13. What will you use as your accent color(s)? _____

    _____

14. Explain your color choices. _____

    _____

    _____

    _____

    _____

    _____

Using the Principles of Design

Golden Guidelines

Activity A   Name _____

Chapter 12   Date _____ Period _____

Answer the questions about the illustrations below.

1. Where did the golden guidelines originate? _____

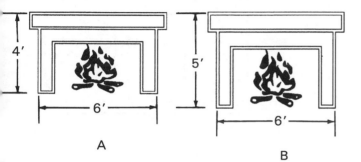

A   B

2. Which of the fireplaces at the left do you find more visually appealing?

   Why? _____

   _____

   _____

3. Which of the golden guidelines is illustrated by fireplace A?

   _____

4. Which of the lamps at the left do you find most visually appealing?

   _____

   Why? _____

   _____

   _____

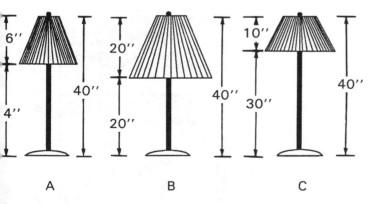

A   B   C

5. Which of the golden guidelines is illustrated by lamp A? _____

6. Which of the picture placements at the left do you find more visually appealing? _____

   Why? _____

   _____

   _____

7. Which of the golden guidelines is illustrated by picture placement B?

   _____

A   B

81

The Principle of Rhythm

Name _____

Date _____ Period _____

Write the type of rhythm illustrated by each of the window treatments shown below. Briefly expla
each type of rhythm.

1. _____
   _____
   _____

2. _____
   _____
   _____

3. _____
   _____
   _____

4. _____
   _____
   _____

5. _____
   _____
   _____

Using the Principles of Design

Activity C

Chapter 12

Name _____

Date _____ Period _____

riefly describe how the principles of design are used in the room illustrated below.

roportion and scale: _____

_____

alance: _____

_____

mphasis: _____

_____

hythm: _____

_____

Design in Reverse

Activity D

Chapter 12

Name_____

Date_____ Period _____

Write a question for each of the following answers based on the content of Chapter 12. Working with three or four of your classmates, take turns asking the questions in a random order. See how many of your group members can answer correctly without looking at the worksheet.

1. Proportion and scale, balance, emphasis, and rhythm.

   _____

2. The relationship of parts of the same object, or the relationship between different objects in the same group.

   _____

3. The golden rectangle, the golden mean, and the golden section.

   _____

4. The relative size of an object in relation to other objects.

   _____

5. Thick lines, bold colors, coarse textures, and large patterns.

   _____

6. Informal balance.

   _____

7. Picture windows, fireplaces, colorful rugs, striking works of art, and mirrors are common examples.

   _____

8. A type of rhythm that is created when an element of design is repeated.

   _____

9. A type of rhythm that is created by a gradual increase or decrease of similar elements of design.

   _____

10. Function and appropriateness, harmony with unity and variety, and beauty.

    _____

11. The result of all parts of a design related by a design idea.

    _____

12. The application of design in regard to the senses of sight, hearing, smell, and touch.

    _____

Textiles in Today's Homes

Facts About Fibers

Activity A

Chapter 13

Name_____

Date_____ Period _____

Select three natural fibers and seven manufactured fibers. Complete the information on the chart, listing two strengths and two weaknesses of each fiber.

Fiber	Characteristics	
	Strengths	Weaknesses
1.	1. 2.	1. 2.
2.	1. 2.	1. 2.
3.	1. 2.	1. 2.
4.	1. 2.	1. 2.
5.	1. 2.	1. 2.
6.	1. 2.	1. 2.
7.	1. 2.	1. 2.
8.	1. 2.	1. 2.
9.	1. 2.	1. 2.
10.	1. 2.	1. 2.

Natural (rows 1–3)

Manufactured (rows 4–10)

Understanding Household Textiles

Activity B

Chapter 13

Name _____

Date _____ Period _____

Mount one example of each—woven, knitted, and nonwoven fabrics—in the spaces provided. Then provide answers to the following questions or statements.

Woven Fabric

1. How are woven fabrics made?_____

_____

2. What are warp yarns? _____

3. What are weft yarns?_____

4. List the three basic weaves. _____

_____

5. Two variations of the plain weave are_____.

6. Long floats (as in satin weave) tend to make a fabric _____ than other basic weaves.

7. In the _____ weave, yarn loops or cut yarns stand away from the fabric base.

8. Fabrics that have a _____ appear different from varying directions.

9. The example above is a _____ weave.

10. List advantages of using this fabric. _____

_____

_____

_____

11. List disadvantages of using this fabric. _____

_____

_____

_____

(Continued)

Knitted Fabric

2. How are knitted fabrics made? _____
_____
_____

3. Why aren't knitted fabrics used as much as woven fabrics in the home? _____
_____
_____

4. What is the major use of knitted fabrics in the home? _____
_____
_____

Nonwoven Fabric

5. List the most common nonwoven fabrics used in the home. _____
_____

6. The example above is a _____

7. What are the advantages of using this fabric? _____
_____
_____

8. What are the disadvantages of using this fabric? _____
_____
_____

Choosing Textiles for the Home

Activity C

Chapter 13

Name _____

Date _____ Period _____

When selecting fabrics for the home several factors are important, but one may be more important tha the others in a specific situation. In the spaces below, briefly describe each factor to consider whe choosing textiles for the home. Then describe a specific situation or household item in which this facto would be the most important factor to consider.

Appearance

Description: _____

Situation/item when this factor would be most important: _____

_____

_____

Durability

Description: _____

Situation/item when this factor would be most important: _____

_____

_____

Maintenance

Description: _____

Situation/item when this factor would be most important: _____

_____

_____

Comfort

Description: _____

Situation/item when this factor would be most important: _____

_____

_____

Ease of use in construction

Description: _____

Situation/item when this factor would be most important: _____

_____

_____

Cost

Description: _____

Situation/item when this factor would be most important: _____

_____

_____

Fabrics for Window Treatments

Name _____

Date _____ Period _____

In the space provided, mount a fabric swatch that could be used for curtains or draperies. Sketch a window treatment appropriate for this fabric. Then provide answers to the following questions or statements.

Fabric:	Window treatment:

1. In what room would this window be located? _____

2. What function would this window treatment serve? _____
   _____

3. Describe the texture of this fabric. _____
   _____

4. Describe the opaqueness of this fabric. _____

5. What is the fiber content of this fabric? _____

6. Describe durability characteristics of this fiber in terms of each of the following:

   A. sunlight resistance _____

   B. abrasion resistance _____

   C. cleaning process _____

   D. other characteristics _____

7. Why is this fabric a good choice for this window treatment? _____
   _____
   _____

Textile Review

Name _____

Date _____ Period _____

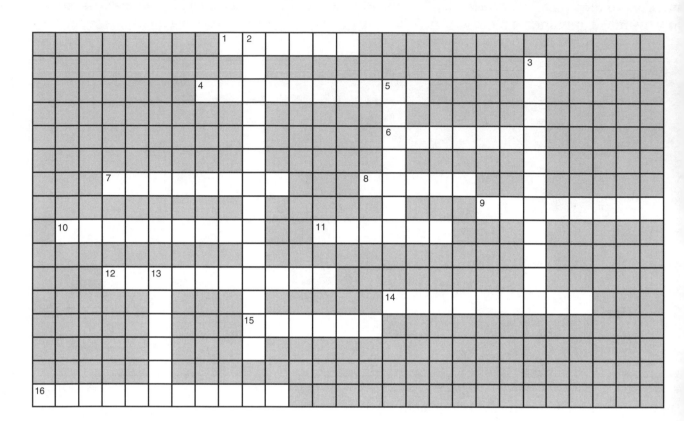

Across

1. A(n) _____ window treatment shuts out light and provides complete privacy.
4. A design made by varying the yarns as the fabric is woven is called a _____ design.
6. A(n) _____ sheet is a high-quality, lightweight, plain-weave bed linen.
7. Treatments applied to fabrics that can improve their appearance, feel, and performance are called _____.
8. The fiber used in making lint-free kitchen towels is _____.
9. Wool that has been used in other products is called _____ wool.
10. A _____ _____ is the largest size bathroom towel.
11. Two layers of fabric permanently joined together with adhesive is a _____ fabric.

12. A(n) _____ finish prevents water from soaking into the fabric.
14. A filled bed covering is a(n) _____.
15. Starch added to provide extra body and weight to fabric is called _____.
16. A _____ _____ is made to follow the shape of a mattress.

Down

2. The _____ _____ finish prevents fabrics from wrinkling.
3. The higher the _____ _____, the more closely woven the fabric is.
5. _____ designs are printed on the surface of the fabric.
13. A(n) _____ carpet has yarn loops secured to the backing with an adhesive.

. . . .

Creating Interior Backgrounds

Floor Treatments

Activity A   Name _____

Chapter 14   Date _____ Period _____

Clip and mount pictures of floor treatments that are appropriate for the indicated areas. Then explain why each choice is appropriate. Give some information about the cost and maintenance of each choice.

Kitchens

1. Living unit with preschoolers

_____
_____
_____
_____
_____
_____
_____
_____

2. Living unit with wheelchair member

_____
_____
_____
_____
_____
_____
_____
_____

(Continued)

Sleeping Area

3. Nursery

_____
_____
_____
_____
_____
_____
_____
_____
_____
_____

4. For teenagers

_____
_____
_____
_____
_____
_____
_____
_____
_____
_____

Wallpaper

Activity B

Chapter 14

Name _____

Date _____ Period _____

Obtain or create two different wallpaper samples. Mount them in the spaces provided and complete the following descriptions.

Color harmony: _____

Ideal location: _____

Mood/feeling conveyed: _____

Ideal supporting colors: _____

_____

Suggested furnishings: _____

_____

_____

Color harmony: _____

Ideal location: _____

Mood/feeling conveyed: _____

Ideal supporting colors: _____

_____

Suggested furnishings: _____

_____

_____

Backgrounds Crossword

Name _____

Date _____ Period _____

(Continued

Across

1. Drywall or _____ _____ is the most common material used for interior walls.
4. _____ is a type of ceiling plaster or tile that helps absorb sound.
7. A room can appear twice its size if a _____ is used as a wall treatment.
10. _____ is a practical wall treatment available in a variety of patterns or scenes.
13. As a wall treatment, _____ can add color, warmth, texture, and interest to a room.
16. _____ paint is usually the least expensive type of paint.
17. A _____ wall treatment is one that never goes out of style.
18. _____ tile is a hard, durable covering for both floors and walls.
21. _____ paint withstands washing and scrubbing the best.
23. Southern yellow pine, Douglas fir, hemlock, and larch are common for _____ floors.
25. An _____ rug can be placed to define a part of a room.
26. Applying _____ to walls requires special skills and usually is expensive.
27. Although resistant to stains, a _____ floor covering can be damaged by abrasion.
29. _____ floors are made of a mixture of cement and marble chips.
31. _____ is usually made of plywood and is appropriate for any room.

Down

2. _____ is the fastest and least expensive wall treatment.
3. Semigloss paint is sometimes called _____ paint.
5. Clay or _____ tile is a strong and durable floor material found in natural colors such as golds, reds, grays, blacks, and browns.
6. _____ tile is great for foot comfort and controlling sound, but it wears rapidly and dents easily.
8. _____ is commonly used as a floor material because of its beauty, warmth, and durability.
9. The _____ is usually the first background that is planned in a room.
11. Before choosing a _____ treatment, consider the personalities of the people who use the room.
12. Using _____ extends the indoor space and brings the outdoors in.
14. _____ is a floor material often used for some entries, basements, and garages.
15. _____-_____-_____ carpeting covers an entire floor, making rooms appear larger and more luxurious.
19. A _____-_____ rug exposes a small border of floor.
20. _____ wallboard is used mostly in bathrooms and kitchens.
22. _____ floor treatments are those that have some "give" but retain their original shape.
24. Paint colors will appear _____ when they are applied to walls.
28. _____ is costly to install, but is durable and easy to maintain.
30. _____ floors are beautiful, durable, and costly. They look best in informal settings.

Backgrounds

Name _____

Date _____ Period _____

Select a picture of a room with a background design that has influenced the way the rest of the room ha▪
been decorated. Attach the picture in the space provided and answer the questions that follow.

1. Why do you think the floor treatment was selected for this room? _____
   _____

2. Why do you think the wall treatment was selected for this room? _____
   _____
   _____

3. How have the backgrounds influenced the way the rest of this room has been decorated? _____
   _____
   _____
   _____

4. If the backgrounds remained the same, in what ways would they limit the types of changes tha▪
   could be made in this room? _____
   _____
   _____
   _____

5. How would you have treated the floors and/or walls in this room? Explain. _____
   _____
   _____

Furniture Styles and Construction

Furniture Styles

Activity A

Chapter 15

Name_____

Date_____ Period _____

Identify each of these furniture styles and arrange them into the three groupings by indicating the letter and the name of the style in the chart on the next page. Then match each style to its description.

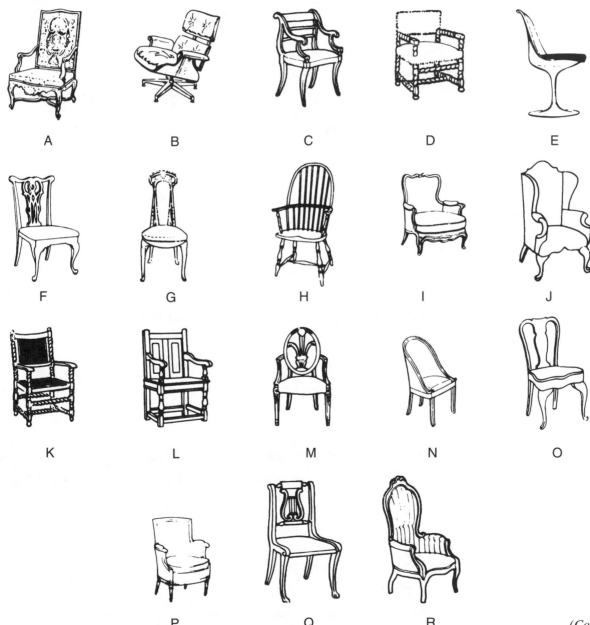

A

B

C

D

E

F

G

H

I

J

K

L

M

N

O

P

Q

R

(Continued)

French		English		American	
Letter	Style name	Letter	Style name	Letter	Style name

_____ 1. Excessive use of ornamentation and massive proportions.

_____ 2. Turning and fluting on oak furniture.

_____ 3. Extravagant furniture with heavy ornamentation and gold overlays.

_____ 4. Lyre motif backs, brass-tipped dog feet, curved legs, and rolled-top rails.

_____ 5. Dignified style made popular by Napoleon.

_____ 6. Simple, straight lines and classic motifs, such as fluted columns.

_____ 7. Grand and formal furniture style with carving and rich inlays.

_____ 8. Splat-back chairs with curved top edges.

_____ 9. Based on England's Georgian style; has graceful lines and S-shaped legs.

_____ 10. Graceful lines based on flower forms; considered "new art" at the time.

_____ 11. An example of Early American furniture; usually made from maple, pine, and oak.

_____ 12. Graceful and comfortable with cabriole legs and carved fans and shells.

_____ 13. Molded plastic design.

_____ 14. Delicate with curved lines, soft colors, and smaller proportions.

_____ 15. Bold, curved lines, which reflect an interest in the ancient cultures of Greece, Rome, ar Egypt.

_____ 16. Molded rosewood, vinyl cushions, and chrome base.

_____ 17. Graceful lines with shield, oval, and heart shapes as well as delicately carved splats.

_____ 18. A practical chair built by the first settlers in America; a simplified version of tl Jacobean style.

Materials Make the Furniture

Name _____

Date _____ Period _____

Below are listed six categories of materials that can be used in furniture. For each category, try to list as many pieces of furniture as possible that use the material as part of their structure.

Wood	
Plastic	
Metal	
Rattan and Wicker	
Glass	
Fabric	

Wood Joints

Name _____

Date _____ Period _____

Identify the wood joints pictured. Then match each joint to two descriptions below.

A. _____   B. _____   C. _____

D. _____   E. _____   F. _____

_____ 1. This joint is used where several boards are joined lengthwise.

_____ 2. For this type of joint, one board is simply glued or nailed flush to another.

_____ 3. This joint has glued wooden dowels which fit into holes that have been drilled in bot
pieces of wood.

_____ 4. This joint is invisible if done skillfully.

_____ 5. This joint supports and reinforces the furniture frame.

_____ 6. This is the weakest of all joints.

_____ 7. This is one of the strongest joints used for furniture.

_____ 8. This type of joint is used to fasten pieces of wood that meet at right angles by cutting a
interlocking pattern in both pieces.

_____ 9. This type of joint is found in drawers of good-quality furniture.

_____ 10. This joint is constructed by tightly fitting a piece of wood with a notch in it to a piece
wood with a hole cut to match the notch.

_____ 11. This joint keeps one side of the furniture from pulling away from the other side.

_____ 12. Because two separate pieces of wood are fitted into the two pieces to be joined, this join
is very strong.

Shopping for Upholstered Furniture

Activity D

Chapter 15

Name _____

Date _____ Period _____

isit a furniture or department store. Choose a piece of furniture and evaluate it by completing the uestions below. Read the labels to find the information or ask a salesperson for assistance. Sketch the irniture piece in the space provided, or clip and mount a picture from an ad.

1. Are the legs and joints securely attached? _____

2. What kind of springs have been used? _____

3. From what materials were the cushions made? _____

   _____

4. Are the cushions reversible? _____

5. Does the outer covering have a well-tailored appearance? _____

6. Is the outer covering made of a woven, nonwoven, or knitted fabric? _____

7. Will the fiber and construction of the outer covering provide good wearability? _____

   _____

8. Does the outer covering have a soil/stain-resistant finish? _____

9. If a sleeper sofa, is it comfortable and convenient for both sitting and sleeping? _____

   _____

0. In what type of room would this piece of furniture be appropriate? _____

   _____

   _____

1. How does the quality of the furniture and the price compare? _____

   _____

Furniture Advertisements

Name_____

Date_____ **Period** _____

Clip and mount an advertisement that pictures and describes furniture. Analyze the advertisement b
completing the statements below.

Helpful information given in the advertisement:

_____

_____

_____

_____

_____

Information not given in the advertisement:

_____

_____

_____

_____

_____

Questions I would ask a sales associate about the furniture advertised:

_____

_____

_____

_____

· ·

Arranging and Selecting Furniture

Arranging Furniture in a Bedroom

Activity A   Name _____

Chapter 16   Date _____ Period _____

Design a bedroom for a teenager. Draw the bedroom to scale on the graph paper below. Choose appropriate furniture from the furniture templates on pages 107 and 108, and arrange it on your plan. Then complete an evaluation of the bedroom on the next page.

Scale: ¼ inch = 1 foot

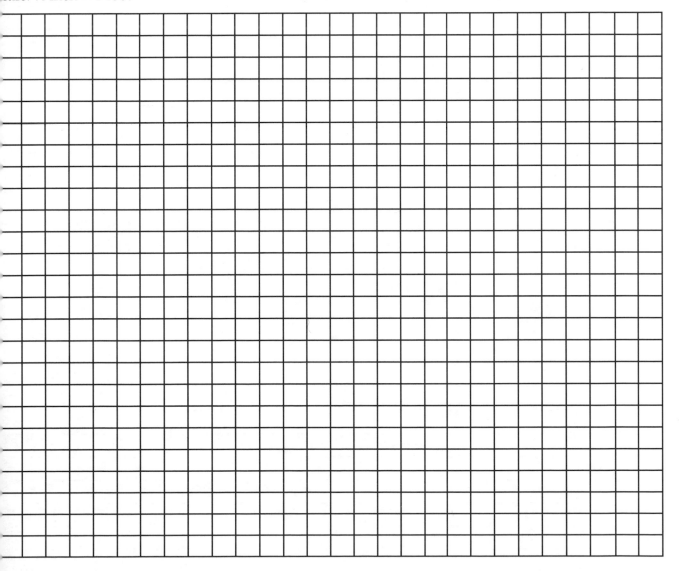

(Continued)

Floor Plan Evaluation

Analyze your floor plan by checking the appropriate responses below:

	Yes	No
Adequate furniture for sleeping	_____	_____
Adequate furniture and space for relaxation	_____	_____
Adequate clearance space allowed around furniture	_____	_____
Adequate furniture and space for studying	_____	_____
Adequate space for dressing	_____	_____
Adequate closet space	_____	_____
Adequate drawer space	_____	_____
Adequate space for grooming	_____	_____
Adequate storage for grooming supplies	_____	_____
No interference from furniture arrangement with the features of the room	_____	_____
Enough space in the furniture arrangement for people to move about freely	_____	_____

Do you believe this room is functional? Explain. _____

_____

_____

_____

_____

_____

_____

_____

_____

_____

_____

_____

_____

_____

_____

_____

_____

_____

_____

_____

_____

_____

Arranging the Social Area

Name _____

Date _____ Period _____

Design the social area(s) of a house for a young couple that does a great deal of entertaining. Describe the social area and draw it to scale on the graph below. Choose appropriate furniture pieces from the furniture template on pages 107 and 108 and arrange them on your plan. Then complete an evaluation of your plan on the next page.

Description: _____

Scale: ¼ inch = 1 foot

(Continued)

Floor Plan Evaluation

Analyze your floor plan by checking the appropriate responses in the chart and answering the question below.

	Yes	No
Adequate furniture and space for daily living.	_____	_____
Adequate furniture and space for entertaining	_____	_____
Adequate furniture and space for recreation (optional)	_____	_____
Adequate furniture and space for dining (optional)	_____	_____
Adequate entry for greeting guests.	_____	_____
Adequate storage for outerwear and other items requiring storage in the area	_____	_____
Adequate clearance space allowed around furniture	_____	_____
No interruption of activities within the room from traffic pattern.	_____	_____
Convenient and direct traffic patterns	_____	_____
No interference from furniture arrangement with the features of the room	_____	_____
Enough space in the furniture arrangement to allow people to move about freely . .	_____	_____

Do you believe this area is functional? Explain. _____

_____

_____

_____

_____

_____

_____

_____

_____

_____

_____

_____

_____

_____

_____

_____

_____

_____

_____

_____

Furniture Template

race onto another sheet of paper the furniture pieces you plan to use in the rooms you have designed.
hen cut out the pieces, arrange them, and glue them in place on your floor plan.

cale: ¼ inch = 1 foot

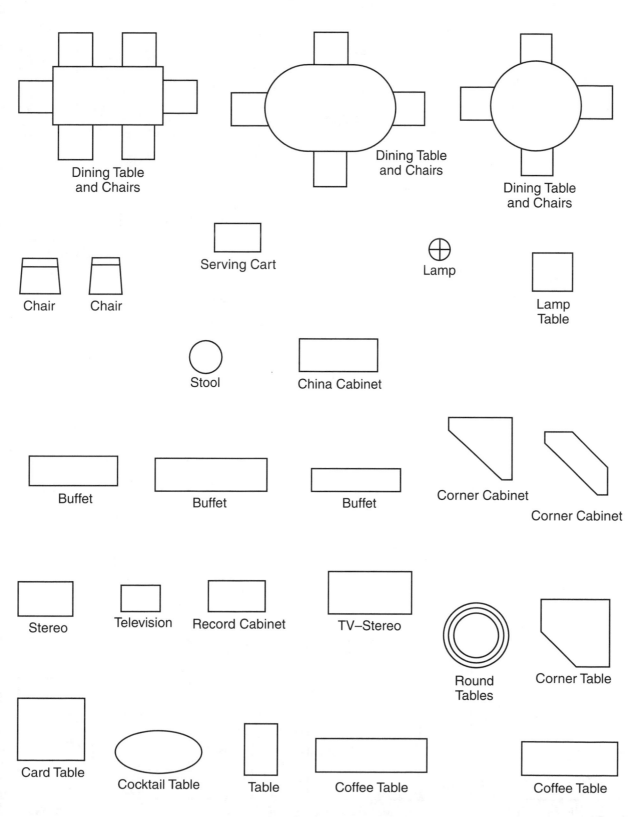

Dining Table and Chairs

Dining Table and Chairs

Dining Table and Chairs

Serving Cart

Lamp

Chair   Chair

Lamp Table

Stool   China Cabinet

Buffet   Buffet   Buffet   Corner Cabinet   Corner Cabinet

Stereo   Television   Record Cabinet   TV–Stereo   Round Tables   Corner Table

Card Table   Cocktail Table   Table   Coffee Table   Coffee Table

(Continued)

Sofa

Love Seat

Lounge
Chair

Sofa
Sections

Piano

Arm-
chair

Arm-
chair

Ottoman

Ottoman

Ottoman

Piano

Storage

Storage

Storage

Bookcase

Bookcase

Bookcase

Chest

Chest

Dressing Table

Desk

Chest

Chest

Night
Table

Night
Table

Night
Table

Chest

Chest

Chest

Chest

Chest

King-Size Bed

Queen-Size Bed

Double Bed

Twin Bed

Deciding Where to Shop for Furniture

Name_____

Date_____ Period _____

Visit four different stores that sell furniture. Try to include a furniture store, a department store, and a warehouse showroom. List each store's name and the type of store it is. Then list the services available at each. Also compare the prices and quality of similar items.

Store 1

Name:_____Type:_____

Services available: _____

_____

Prices of furniture:_____

Quality of furniture: _____

Store 2

Name:_____Type:_____

Services available: _____

_____

Prices of furniture:_____

Quality of furniture: _____

Store 3

Name:_____Type:_____

Services available: _____

_____

Prices of furniture:_____

Quality of furniture: _____

Store 4

Name:_____Type:_____

Services available: _____

_____

Prices of furniture:_____

Quality of furniture: _____

Where would you prefer to purchase furniture? Explain. _____

_____

Bargain Brochure

Activity D

Chapter 16

Name _____

Date _____ Period _____

Design a pamphlet that explains to consumers some of the advantages, as well as the pitfalls, of purchasing items at significantly lower prices. Use this page to write a draft of the information you wil include in the brochure.

Let the Buyer Beware

Introduction: _____

_____

_____

_____

_____

Loss leader sales: _____

_____

_____

_____

_____

Seasonal sales: _____

_____

_____

_____

_____

Close-out sales: _____

_____

_____

_____

_____

Slightly damaged/discontinued items: _____

_____

_____

_____

_____

Garage sales, auctions, flea markets: _____

_____

_____

_____

_____

Comparing Information Sources for Buying Furniture

Activity E

Chapter 16

Name _____

Date _____ Period _____

Find an example of each of the furniture information sources listed below. Describe the types of information provided by each source. If possible, attach the advertisement and label to this page. Photocopy the magazine articles you use for this assignment and also attach them to this page. Then answer the questions that follow.

Book or Magazine

Title: _____

Information provided: _____

_____

_____

Consumer Reports Article

Title: _____

Information provided: _____

_____

_____

Newpaper or Magazine Advertisement

Title: _____

Information provided: _____

_____

_____

Furniture Label

Information provided: _____

_____

_____

Which information source was most useful? _____

Why? _____

_____

_____

What other types of information are beneficial for buyers of furniture to use?

_____

_____

_____

Test Your Knowledge

Name _____

Date _____ Period _____

Prepare a question about furniture and provide its answer for each of the topics listed below.

1. "Room arrangement" question: _____

   _____

   Answer: _____

   _____

2. "Prioritizing needs" question: _____

   _____

   Answer: _____

   _____

3. "What is affordable" question: _____

   _____

   Answer: _____

   _____

4. "Where to buy" question: _____

   _____

   Answer: _____

   _____

5. "When to buy" question: _____

   _____

   Answer: _____

   _____

6. "Information sources" question: _____

   _____

   Answer: _____

   _____

7. "Finding bargains" question: _____

   _____

   Answer: _____

   _____

8. "Reusing furniture" question: _____

   _____

   Answer: _____

Addressing Windows, Lighting, and Accessories

Choosing Window Treatments

Activity A

Chapter 17

Name _____

Date _____ Period _____

Identify a window treatment that is appropriate for each window style shown below. Draw the window treatments on the windows. Compare your answers with your classmates.

1. _____

2. _____

3. _____

4. _____

5. _____

6. _____

Measuring for Window Treatments

Name _____

Date _____ Period _____

Describe in your own words how to measure windows for draw draperies, curtains, and cafe curtains. Use labels wherever they would make your descriptions clearer.

Draw Draperies

_____
_____
_____
_____
_____
_____

Curtains

_____
_____
_____
_____
_____

Cafe Curtains

_____
_____
_____
_____
_____
_____

Lighting for Activities

Activity C

Chapter 17

Name_____

Date_____ Period _____

ist various activities that might be carried out in the following rooms. Then look through magazines
nd clip and mount pictures of lighting fixtures appropriate for the rooms. Indicate the minimum recommended footcandles of light needed in the space provided. (To determine the minimum recom-
ended footcandles, use chart 17-21 of the text.)

Kitchen

Activities: _____

_____

Minimum recommended footcandles:

Bedroom

Activities: _____

_____

Minimum recommended footcandles:

(Continued)

Utility Room/Workshop

Activities: _____

_____

Minimum recommended footcandles of light:

Dining Room

Activities: _____

_____

Minimum recommended footcandles of light:

Bathroom

Activities: _____

_____

Minimum recommended footcandles of light:

Lighting for Safety

Name _____

Date _____ Period _____

n the floor plan, indicate where light switches should be located for safe lighting. Then place a check
the blank next to each statement below that describes lighting planned for safety.

_____ 1. Entrances are well lighted.

_____ 2. Garage/carport lighting is controlled from the house.

_____ 3. Lamps have the Underwriters Laboratories seal, indicating they were manufactured according to safety standards.

_____ 4. You must walk across the room to switch the lights on or off.

_____ 5. Stairway lighting can be controlled from both the top and bottom of the stairs.

_____ 6. Entrances are dark.

_____ 7. Garage/carport lighting is dim.

_____ 8. Extra electrical circuits are available so no overloading will occur.

_____ 9. Room lighting can be switched on or off from each doorway.

_____ 10. Stairway lighting can be controlled only at the base of the stairs.

_____ 11. One electrical socket is overused while nearby sockets go unused.

_____ 12. All wiring complies with the National Electrical Code.

_____ 13. Outside lighting can be controlled from inside the house.

_____ 14. All lighting fixtures are installed according to the manufacturer's directions.

Structural and Nonstructural Lighting

Activity E   Name _____

Chapter 17   Date _____ Period _____

Check magazines for two examples of nonstructural lighting and three examples of structural lighting. Clip and mount the pictures in the appropriate spaces. Then analyze the lighting by providing the information requested.

Nonstructural lighting example 1:	Lighting type: _____
	Type of light provided (check all that apply):
	____diffused light ____specific lighting
	____direct lighting ____lighting for safety
	____indirect lighting ____accent lighting
	____general lighting
	Room(s) appropriate for this type of lighting:
	_____
	_____

Nonstructural lighting example 2:	Lighting type: _____
	Type of light provided (check all that apply):
	____diffused light ____specific lighting
	____direct lighting ____lighting for safety
	____indirect lighting ____accent lighting
	____general lighting
	Room(s) appropriate for this type of lighting:
	_____
	_____

(Continued)

Name _____

Structural lighting example 1:	Lighting type: _____
	Type of light provided (check all that apply):
	____diffused light ____specific lighting
	____direct lighting ____lighting for safety
	____indirect lighting ____accent lighting
	____general lighting
	Room(s) appropriate for this type of lighting:
	_____
	_____

Structural lighting example 2:	Lighting type: _____
	Type of light provided (check all that apply):
	____diffused light ____specific lighting
	____direct lighting ____lighting for safety
	____indirect lighting ____accent lighting
	____general lighting
	Room(s) appropriate for this type of lighting:
	_____
	_____

Structural lighting example 3:	Lighting type: _____
	Type of light provided (check all that apply):
	____diffused light ____specific lighting
	____direct lighting ____lighting for safety
	____indirect lighting ____accent lighting
	____general lighting
	Room(s) appropriate for this type of lighting:
	_____
	_____

Accessories

Activity F

Chapter 17

Name _____

Date _____ Period _____

In the space provided, mount a magazine picture showing a good use of accessories in a room. Then lis
each accessory in the appropriate column below and answer the following question.

Functional Accessories	Decorative Accessories	Dual-Purpose Accessories

Considering color, style, and purpose, how do these accessories tie the room's furnishings together?

_____

_____

_____

_____

_____

_____

. . . .

Selecting Household Equipment

Choosing Major Appliances

Activity A   Name_____

Chapter 18   Date_____ Period _____

Write eight questions that will help a person carefully select a new major appliance. Mount a catalog picture of a major appliance and its description in the space provided. Relate your questions to the pictured appliance and write the answers below.

Appliance Questions

1. _____
2. _____
3. _____
4. _____
5. _____
6. _____
7. _____
8. _____

Appliance Answers

1. _____
2. _____
3. _____
4. _____
5. _____
6. _____
7. _____
8. _____

Refrigerators

Name_____

Date_____ Period _____

In the space provided, mount pictures of newspaper ads or catalogs showing the four refrigerator models named. For each model, list the price, one advantage, and one disadvantage. Then answer the question that follows.

One-door, full-size model: Price: _____ Advantage:_____ Disadvantage: _____ _____	**Two-door, side-by-side model:** Price: _____ Advantage: _____ Disadvantage: _____ _____
Two-door, side-by-side model with dispenser feature: Price: _____ Advantage:_____ Disadvantage: _____ _____	**Two-door, top-freezer model:** Price: _____ Advantage: _____ _____ Disadvantage:_____ _____

Which of the above models do you prefer? Explain your answer.

_____

_____

_____

_____

_____

_____

Microwave Ovens

Activity C　　　　　　　　　Name _____

Chapter 18　　　　　　　　　Date _____ Period _____

Visit an appliance dealer or the appliance department of a local store. Compare two different models of microwave ovens using the form below. Then answer the questions that follow.

	Model 1	Model 2
1. Manufacturer	_____	_____
2. Style	_____	_____
3. Oven capacity	_____	_____
4. Oven wattage	_____	_____
5. Number of power levels	_____	_____
6. Automatic programming	_____	_____
7. Automatic settings	_____	_____
8. Browning element	_____	_____
9. Temperature probe or food sensor	_____	_____
10. Turntable	_____	_____
11. Microwave cookbook	_____	_____

Which features do you consider most important in a microwave oven? Why? _____

_____

_____

_____

_____

Which of the models described above do you prefer? Why? _____

_____

_____

_____

_____

_____

_____

_____

_____

Washers and Dryers

Name _____

Date _____ Period _____

Obtain use and care manuals for an automatic washer and dryer from home, from an appliance store or by contacting an appliance manufacturer. Use the manuals to fill out the checklists and answer the questions below. For the checklists, place **Y** in the blanks for *yes*, and **N** for *no*.

Checklist for Automatic Washers

___Will the washer fit your space limitations?

___Does the washer have a self-cleaning lint filter?

___Is a water-level selector provided if the model is top-loading?

___Is a water temperature selector provided?

___Is more than one cycle available, including a presoak cycle? A permanent-press cycle? A knit cycle? A delicate cycle?

___Does it have a control to stop the machine and signal when the load is unbalanced?

___Are bleach, fabric softener, and detergent dispensers offered?

___Is an optional second rinse selector provided?

___Is the tub and lid made of porcelain enamel?

What other information in the manual would help you decide about purchasing this washer? Explain.

_____

_____

Checklist for Dryers

___Is the lint trap conveniently placed for ease in removing, cleaning, and replacing?

___Is the control panel lighted? The interior?

___Is there a signal (buzzer or bell) at the end of the drying period?

___Is there a safety button to start the dryer?

___Does the dryer offer one heat setting or a choice?

___Does it have an automatic sensor to prevent overdrying?

___Does it offer a wrinkle-guard feature? An air-only, no-heat setting?

___Does it have a touch-up cycle to remove creases in dry clothes?

What other information in the manual would help you decide about purchasing this dryer? Explain.

_____

_____

_____

_____

_____

_____

_____

_____

_____

Appliance Puzzler

Activity E

Chapter 18

Name _____

Date _____ Period _____

Complete the following sentences by placing the missing word(s) in the preceding blanks.

_____ 1. _____ labels state the average yearly energy use and operating cost of an appliance.

_____ 2. For safety, appliances should have a seal from a reputable safety-testing organization such as _____ _____.

_____ 3. Under a(n) _____ warranty, you may have the item repaired or replaced free of charge (at the warrantor's option).

_____ 4. Under a(n) _____ warranty, you can be charged for repairs.

_____ 5. When shopping for a(n) _____, you should consider how much storage space you need and whether or not you need a separate freezer section.

_____ 6. A(n) _____ can help save you money if you use it to store food purchased at low prices.

_____ 7. Large, bulky packages are easier to store in a(n) _____ freezer.

_____ 8. Food is easier to see and remove in a(n) _____ freezer.

_____ 9. A(n) _____ freezer prevents the build-up of frost, but the purchase and operation cost is more.

_____ 10. A kitchen _____ may be fueled by electricity or gas.

_____ 11. A(n) _____ cooktop uses a magnetic field to generate heat.

_____ 12. A(n) _____ range is the most common type.

_____ 13. A(n) _____-_____ range, with the oven below the cooking surface, fits snugly between two base cabinets.

_____ 14. A(n) _____-_____ range has a cooking surface separate from the oven to allow flexible kitchen arrangements.

_____ 15. A range _____ is used over the cooking surface to help vent heat and odors from the kitchen

_____ 16. _____-_____ ovens, which have extra insulation, can be set at extremely high temperatures to "burn" spills and spatters away.

_____ 17. _____-cleaning ovens have a special coating on the oven walls which oxidizes food spatters over a period of time during the normal baking process.

_____ 18. _____ ovens require about two-thirds the time and half the energy of conventional cooking because a fan circulates the heat.

_____ 19. _____ ovens can save up to 75 percent of the energy used by conventional ovens when cooking certain foods.

(Continued)

Name _____

_____ 20. A(n) _____ can clean dishes better than hand-washing can.

_____ 21. A trash _____ can compress household trash to about one-fourth its origina volume.

_____ 22. The smell and mess of food scraps are easily eliminated by a food wast _____.

_____ 23. In a(n) _____ _____, all cycles have the same basic steps: wash, rinse, and spin.

_____ 24. Basic _____ models have a preset temperature that is safe for most fabrics.

_____ 25. An insulating _____ can be wrapped around a water heater to provid added insulation.

_____ 26. A(n) _____ vacuum cleaner is good for cleaning stairs and upholstery.

_____ 27. _____ is a program of instructions that tells a computer what to do.

_____ 28. _____ appliances can be easily moved from one place to another.

The Outdoor Living Space

Landscape Elements

Activity A	**Name**_____
Chapter 19	**Date**_____ **Period**_____

In the space below, clip and mount a picture of a landscaped area. Identify the natural and man-made elements in your illustration.

Natural Landscape Elements

_____

_____

_____

_____

_____

_____

Man-Made Landscape Elements

_____

_____

_____

_____

_____

_____

Landscape Backgrounds

Name _____

Date _____ Period _____

Landscapes have their own floors, walls, and ceilings. Find a picture of a landscaped area in a magazine and mount it in the space below. Then answer the questions on the following page.

(Continued

1. What is the floor of the landscape?

_____

_____

_____

_____

2. List landscape elements used to create the floor.

Natural Landscape Elements   **Man-Made Landscape Elements**

_____   _____

_____   _____

_____   _____

3. What are the walls of the landscape?

_____

_____

_____

_____

4. List landscape elements used to create the walls.

Natural Landscape Elements   **Man-Made Landscape Elements**

_____   _____

_____   _____

_____   _____

5. What creates the ceiling of the landscape?

_____

_____

_____

6. List landscape elements used to create the ceiling.

Natural Landscape Elements   **Man-Made Landscape Elements**

_____   _____

_____   _____

_____   _____

Landscape Accents

Activity C

Chapter 19

Name _____

Date _____ Period _____

Accents in a landscape are the finishing touches. Mount a picture of a landscaped site, or refer to the picture you used for Activity B. Identify the accents used. Then list five suggestions to follow when choosing accents.

Accents Used in the Landscape

_____   _____

_____   _____

_____   _____

_____   _____

Suggestions to Follow When Choosing Landscape Accents

1. _____

   _____

2. _____

   _____

3. _____

   _____

4. _____

   _____

5. _____

   _____

A Look at Outdoor Furnishings

Activity D

Chapter 19

Name _____

Date _____ Period _____

ind three pictures or advertisements for various types of outdoor furnishings. For each, complete the
nformation below.

Example 1

Type:_____

Materials used: _____

Quality features:_____

_____

_____

Use(s): _____

Disadvantages in this item: _____

_____

_____

Example 2

Type:_____

Materials used: _____

Quality features:_____

_____

_____

Use(s): _____

Disadvantages in this item: _____

_____

_____

Example 3

Type:_____

Materials used: _____

Quality features:_____

_____

_____

Use(s): _____

Disadvantages in this item: _____

_____

_____

Designing a Landscape

Name _____

Date _____ Period _____

Design the landscaping for the house shown below. List three goals that you would like to achieve i your landscape plan based on the needs and interests of the people who will live in the house. The sca is ¼″ = 3′.

Goals:

1. _____

2. _____

3. _____

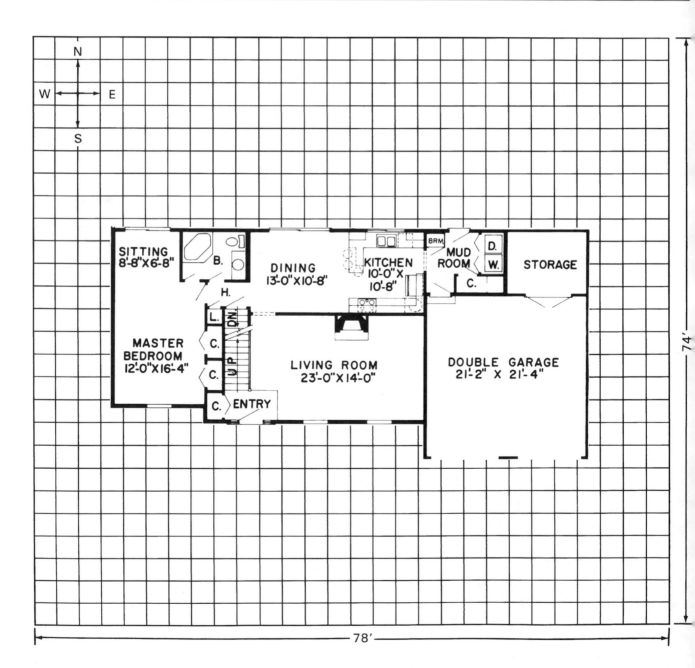

• •

Keeping Your Home Safe and Secure

Causes of Accidents and Safety Measures

Activity A

Chapter 20

Name _____

Date _____ Period _____

List five types of accidents, their probable causes, and safety measures that might prevent the accidents.

Accident	Causes	Safety Measures
1.		
2.		
3.		
4.		
5.		

Clean Air Puzzle

Name_____

Date_____ Period _____

Solve the following word puzzle by filling in the blanks in the statements below.

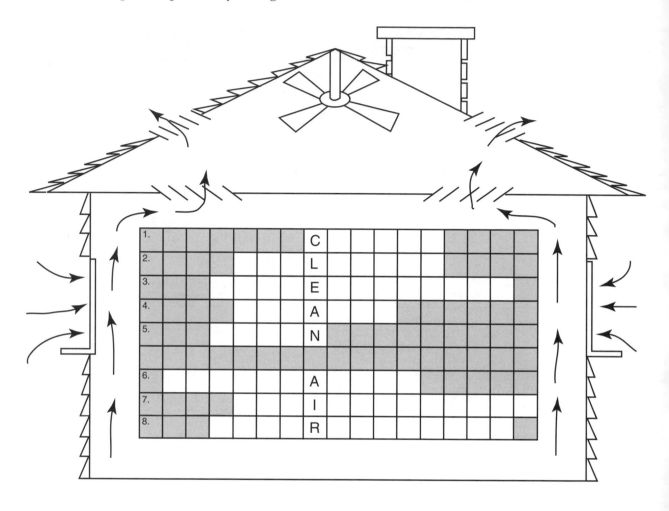

1. A deadly gas produced in a house by poorly maintained gas-burning appliances is _____ monoxide.

2. Inside air _____ in the home is more of a concern today than in the past because houses are more airtight.

3. A _____ _____ sounds an alarm when a fire starts.

4. People who use _____ are adding to indoor air pollution.

5. A natural, dangerous radioactive gas that can be trapped inside the house is known as _____.

6. _____ reduces indoor pollution levels by allowing an exchange of fresh and stale air.

7. The _____ Protection Agency (EPA) is concerned about air quality.

8. A _____ _____ system helps clean the air that is filtered and exhausted to the outside.

Protecting Your Home from Fire

Activity C

Chapter 20

Name _____

Date _____ Period _____

Visit a store or look through catalogs and compare two types of smoke detectors.

	Brand 1: _____	Brand 2: _____
Cost		
Warranty information		
Operation		
Special features		

Which smoke detector would you buy? Explain. _____

_____

_____

_____

_____

List where you would place smoke detectors in a dwelling. Explain. _____

_____

_____

_____

List where you would place fire extinguishers in a dwelling. Explain. _____

_____

_____

_____

_____

_____

A Plan for Fire Emergencies

Activity D

Chapter 20

Name _____

Date _____ Period _____

With the other members of your living unit, decide on an escape plan in case a fire occurs. Draw a floor plan of your entire house or apartment in the space below. Show all possible exits from each room. Mark a main escape route and an alternate route from each room. Then complete the information at the bottom of this page.

1. What signal, such as a loud whistle or a bell, will you use to communicate a fire emergency?

_____

2. Where will everyone meet after you exit the house? _____

_____

3. Does everyone know how to do the door test? Explain here how it is done. _____

_____

_____

4. Who will assist small children or older people who might need assistance? _____

_____

_____

5. What number do you call to reach the fire department in your community? _____

6. What additional practices should you follow in a fire emergency? _____

_____

_____

Home Security Inspection Checklist

Activity E   Name _____

Chapter 20   Date _____ Period_____

Conduct a home security inspection using the checklist below. Then identify any changes that would make your home more secure.

Entrances

_____ Are the doors solid wood construction or metal with secure locks?

_____ Are the door frames strong enough to prevent forced entry?

_____ Does each entrance have a screen or storm door with a secure lock?

_____ Are all entrances well lighted?

_____ Is there an automatic system that lights exterior doors from dusk to dawn or motion-detecting lights?

_____ Can the entrances be observed from the street?

_____ Are all entrances free from concealing landscaping (trees, shrubs, bushes)?

_____ Do the entrances have peepholes or chain locks to permit you to see who is there?

_____ Is there an electronic alarm system?

_____ Do sliding glass doors have extra security devices?

Windows

_____ Do all windows have secure locks in working condition?

_____ Do windows have screens or storm windows that lock from the inside?

_____ Are window areas well lighted and free from concealing landscaping?

Garage Doors and Windows

_____ Is the overhead door equipped with a secure lock? Is the entry door kept closed and locked at all times?

_____ Are tools and ladders stored in the garage, not outside?

_____ Are all doors well lighted on the outside?

(Continued)

Other Security Precautions

_____ Do you leave a vehicle in the driveway when you are away?

_____ Do you keep newspapers picked up each day from around the house?

_____ Do you remove emptied trash cans from the curb right away?

_____ Do you empty your mailbox daily?

_____ Do you have a variable timer to turn lights on and off inside the house automatically?

_____ Do you keep your yard mowed and snow removed from walkways, even when away from home?

_____ Do you open drapes during the day and close them at night?

Review this checklist with the members of your living unit. What security precautions could you take to improve your home security? _____

_____

_____

_____

_____

_____

_____

_____

_____

_____

_____

_____

_____

_____

_____

_____

• •

Maintaining Your Home

Cleaning Tasks

Activity A   Name _____

Chapter 21   Date _____ Period _____

Review the list below. Identify whether the cleaning activity is a daily (**D**), weekly (**W**), monthly (**M**), or semiannual (**S**) task.

_____ 1. Change bed linens.

_____ 2. Wash dishes.

_____ 3. Vacuum upholstered furniture and drapes, and wipe blinds.

_____ 4. Vacuum carpet.

_____ 5. Sweep kitchen floor.

_____ 6. Wash kitchen floor.

_____ 7. Wash windows and mirrors.

_____ 8. Clean drapes thoroughly.

_____ 9. Make bed.

_____10. Vacuum and turn mattress; wash mattress pad.

_____11. Dust and polish furniture.

_____12. Dry-clean or wash bedding.

_____13. Wash or change the liner of the kitchen trash container.

_____14. Clean silverware.

_____15. Clean and wax furniture.

_____16. Wash bathroom floor.

_____17. Clean kitchen shelves.

_____18. Clean closets.

_____19. Wipe kitchen counter and cooking surfaces; clean sink.

_____20. Clean refrigerator, and defrost if needed.

_____21. Replace shelf paper.

_____22. Do laundry and mending.

_____23. Clean woodwork.

_____24. Clean bathroom sink, tub, and toilet.

_____25. Wash bathroom walls.

_____26. Wash all walls.

_____27. Tidy the bedroom, bathroom, and living and eating areas.

_____28. Wash seldom-used glasses and dinnerware.

_____29. Clean range, including oven.

_____30. Empty wastebaskets, ashtrays, and other trash containers.

Repair Work

Name _____

Date _____ Period _____

Visit a home improvement store or research a catalog to itemize the cost of assembling a home repair kit. Plan a basic kit by listing below the name of each item, its main use, and its cost. Then answer the questions that follow.

Item	Use	Cost
_____	_____	_____
_____	_____	_____
_____	_____	_____
_____	_____	_____
_____	_____	_____
_____	_____	_____
_____	_____	_____
_____	_____	_____
_____	_____	_____

Total: _____

1. How should a nail or screw be placed in a wall to hang a picture?

   _____

   _____

   _____

   _____

   _____

   _____

   _____

2. Does the service entrance panel of your home or apartment contain fuses or circuit breakers? When an overload occurs, what procedures and precautions should be followed to restore power?

   _____

   _____

   _____

   _____

   _____

   _____

   _____

   _____

   _____

   _____

Meeting Your Storage Needs

Activity C　　　　　　　　　　　**Name** _____

Chapter 21　　　　　　　　　　　**Date** _____ **Period** _____

Select an area of your home where storage is a problem and describe it. Then answer the questions that follow. If possible, provide pictures of storage items you might use.

Description of storage problem: _____

_____

_____

_____

_____

What items should be stored in this area? _____

_____

_____

What is the current method of storing these items? _____

_____

_____

Describe how you would solve this storage problem. You may want to attach a sketch of your plans.

_____

_____

_____

_____

_____

_____

_____

_____

_____

What storage devices would you use, if any? Attach pictures of these devices, if possible. _____

_____

_____

_____

What is the approximate cost of these devices? _____

Does your plan require any construction skills? If so, describe. _____

_____

_____

_____

_____

Redecorating

Name_____

Date_____ Period _____

Select a magazine picture of an attractive room. Clip and mount the picture below. Then answer the questions in the space provided.

A. How would you change the appearance of this room with a $500 redecorating budget?

_____

_____

_____

_____

_____

_____

_____

_____

_____

_____

B. How would you change the appearance of this room with a $1500 redecorating budget?

_____

_____

_____

_____

_____

_____

_____

_____

_____

_____

· ·

Housing for Tomorrow

Solar Energy

Activity A   Name_____

Chapter 22   Date_____ Period_____

Today, many houses are being built that use solar energy. Contact a company that produces active solar systems for housing in your community.

Advantages: _____

_____

_____

Disadvantages:_____

_____

_____

Types of systems available locally: _____

_____

_____

Features: _____

_____

Cost:_____

_____

Installation time: _____

_____

Maintenance: _____

_____

_____

Factors to consider when adapting an existing dwelling to use solar energy: _____

_____

_____

_____

Additional information: _____

_____

_____

_____

Pollution

Name _____

Date _____ Period _____

Investigate pollution problems in your community. Complete a list of pollution concerns under each of the following categories. Then answer the questions below.

Land

Air

_____   _____
_____   _____
_____   _____
_____   _____

Water

Visual

_____   _____
_____   _____
_____   _____
_____   _____

What can you do to help solve these problems? _____
_____
_____

What can your community do to help solve these problems? _____
_____
_____

What can government organizations do to help solve these problems? _____
_____
_____

What is your community doing to recycle and reuse waste products? _____
_____

Planning a Community

Name _____

Date _____ Period _____

Working in small groups, plan a community for 25,000 people. Briefly describe the community. Then consider and describe the following factors as they relate to the community you have planned.

Community description:

_____

_____

_____

_____

_____

_____

_____

_____

_____

1. Lifestyles of the occupants:_____

_____

_____

_____

_____

2. Price range of housing: _____

_____

_____

_____

_____

3. Access to schools, religious buildings, stores, and health facilities: _____

_____

_____

_____

_____

4. Recreational facilities: _____

_____

_____

_____

_____

(Continued)

5. Neighborhoods: _____

_____

_____

_____

_____

6. Public transportation system:_____

_____

_____

_____

_____

7. Employment opportunities: _____

_____

_____

_____

_____

8. Educational opportunities: _____

_____

_____

_____

_____

9. Health care facilities: _____

_____

_____

_____

_____

10. Communication systems: _____

_____

_____

_____

_____

Future Housing

Name _____

Date _____ Period _____

Current trends can be used to predict housing might change in the future. In the chart below, list some current trends. Then predict possible effects of these trends on future housing.

Trends Involving People	
Trend	Effect on housing

Trends Involving Environment	
Trend	Effect on housing

Trends Involving Building Materials	
Trend	Effect on housing

Trends Involving Technology	
Trend	Effect on housing

Housing: Today and Tomorrow

Activity E

Chapter 22

Name_____

Date_____ Period _____

Complete the following statements by placing the missing word(s) in preceding blanks.

_____ 1. SMART houses feature an automation system based on _____ technology.

_____ 2. _____ sources of energy replenish themselves regularly.

_____ 3. Almost 20 percent of the world's electricity is supplied by _____ energy.

_____ 4. Waterpower converted to electricity is known as _____ power.

_____ 5. A(n) _____ solar system converts the sun's energy into electricity.

_____ 6. _____ energy comes from steam, hot water, or very hot rock stored deep beneath the surface of the earth.

_____ 7. _____ is the relationship between all living things and their surroundings.

_____ 8. Solid waste placed in _____ can cause toxic substances to seep into groundwater stores.

_____ 9. _____ in pipe connections can enter drinking water as a corrosion byproduct

_____ 10. Signboards, debris, and the destruction of natural surroundings are examples of _____ pollution.

_____ 11. The most preferred method of handling waste is _____ _____.

_____ 12. _____ communities are described as "one-stop living" and are made as self-sufficient as possible.

_____ 13. _____ housing is high density housing, but it allows more space for parks.

_____ 14. A goal of _____ is to test life support systems for future space colonies.

_____ 15. Paolo Soleri's first home was a(n) _____ house.

. . . .

Careers in Housing

Career Cluster

Activity A   Name _____

Chapter 23   Date _____ Period _____

research a housing career area. In the space below, design a career cluster similar to those presented in your textbook. Identify the career cluster, subclusters, and related jobs in your community.

Job Description

Name_____

Date_____ Period _____

Research a specific job by using the publications or resources suggested in the text. Find the following information.

Job: _____

Publications/resources used:_____

_____

Job title definition: _____

_____

_____

List of duties: _____

_____

_____

_____

Personal qualifications needed:_____

_____

_____

_____

Education and training needed: _____

_____

_____

How and where to receive the education and training needed: _____

_____

_____

Future outlook on employment: _____

_____

Earnings potential: _____

_____

Opportunities for advancement: _____

_____

How and where to find this type of job: _____

_____

_____

Related careers: _____

_____

_____

Job and Title Match

Activity C

Chapter 23

Name _____

Date _____ Period _____

Match the job descriptions with the job titles. Then look through the classified ads section of a newspaper and attach job ads below for two of the job titles listed on this page.

Job Descriptions

_____ 1. Locates corners and boundaries of tracts of land.

_____ 2. Does precision work while shaping materials in miniature; may be self-employed.

_____ 3. Designs the strength and safety features for buildings. Must have a bachelor of science degree with courses in mathematics, blueprint reading, drafting, and physics.

_____ 4. Prepares the detailed working drawings used by a builder.

_____ 5. Plans and supervises the design and arrangement of building interiors and furnishings. Works from blueprints to make floor plans to scale and to prepare elevation drawings.

_____ 6. Designs buildings, making sure the proper materials are used and the builder follows the plans. A bachelor's degree and a two-day examination are required before licensing.

_____ 7. Handles the design, selection, and placement of exterior building features, such as trees, shrubs, walkways, parking lots, and open areas.

_____ 8. Must be licensed and familiar with the community, real estate laws, banking laws, and building codes to sell real estate.

Job Titles

A. interior designer

B. model maker

C. architect

D. surveyor

E. drafter

F. real estate agent

G. engineer

H. landscape architect

Advertisement 1

Job title: _____

Advertisement 2

Job title: _____

Personal Qualifications and Careers

Activity D

Chapter 23

Name _____

Date _____ Period _____

Answer the following questions about your personal qualifications and career preference.

Personal Qualifications

1. What kinds of hobbies, activities, or clubs do you enjoy? _____

_____

_____

2. How would you rate yourself (good, fair, poor) in the following areas?

Mathematics: _____ Vocational classes (specify which)

Science: _____ _____: _____

Art: _____ _____: _____

3. Do you prefer heavy physical activity, light physical activity, or desk work? _____

4. Do you like to work with equipment and build things? _____

5. Are you willing to continue your education after high school? _____

What type of continuing education program (vocational school, apprenticeship program, two-year college, four-year college, etc.) most interests you? _____

6. Do you enjoy being outdoors or would you rather stay inside? _____

7. Do you prefer to work regular hours or have a varied schedule? _____

8. Do you prefer to work with a group of coworkers, with one or two people, or alone? _____

_____

9. Do you prefer to lead a group or be a group member? _____

Career Preference

Using your answers to the above questions as a guideline, name a housing career that appeals to you. Give reasons for your choice.

_____

_____

_____

_____

_____

_____

_____

_____

_____

Leadership As a Job Qualification

Name _____

Date _____ Period _____

Leadership skills are needed in all careers. Explain how you would handle the following situations if you were the leader.

Situation #1

You are the architect who is overseeing construction of a new house. You have promised your clients that the house would be ready in April. Simon, the contractor that you hired to supervise construction of the house, is two months behind schedule. When you ask him why, he explains that he is having trouble getting some of the specified building materials because of a trucker's strike. The homeowners do not want a substitution in materials, yet their apartment lease expires in April. How would you handle the situation?

_____

_____

_____

_____

_____

_____

_____

_____

_____

_____

_____

_____

_____

_____

_____

_____

_____

_____

_____

_____

_____

_____

_____

_____

(Continued)

Situation #2

You are leading a team of interior designers consisting of Sergio, Bridgette, and yourself. Your goal is to decorate a home for a French diplomat, and you are meeting to discuss ideas. Sergio, with seven years of experience as a designer, believes his is the best decorating plan to follow. Bridgette only has two years of experience, but she studied interior design for one year in France. So far, she has remained quiet during the meeting. How can you get Bridgette to contribute her ideas? How can you get Sergio to consider ideas other than his own?

_____

_____

_____

_____

_____

_____

_____

_____

_____

_____

_____

_____

_____

_____

_____

_____

_____

_____

_____

_____

_____

_____

_____

_____

_____

_____

_____

_____

_____

Housing Careers Challenge

Activity F

Chapter 23

Name _____

Date _____ Period _____

Complete the following sentences by placing the missing word(s) in the preceding blanks.

_____ 1. Jobs or careers that are closely related make up a career _____.

_____ 2. Sometimes a career cluster is called a career _____.

_____ 3. Important publications about job descriptions and trends are available from the U.S. Department of _____.

_____ 4. A job _____ explains what type of work a particular job involves.

_____ 5. A person who designs safe, attractive, and useful buildings is an _____.

_____ 6. A(n) _____ architect plans the placement of trees, shrubs, walkways, parking lots, and open areas around buildings.

_____ 7. From an architect's sketches and instructions, a(n) _____ prepares the detailed working drawings used by the builder.

_____ 8. A(n) _____ _____ builds a scale model of a project to help an architect's clients visualize large projects.

_____ 9. Using various tools, the _____ locates corners and boundaries of tracts of land.

_____ 10. _____ are housing professionals with a bachelor's degree who work on the safety, strength, and reliability of the structure and its systems.

_____ 11. Estimators, masons, carpenters, plumbers, plasterers, electricians, drywallers, roofers, and flooring specialists are all examples of people with _____ careers.

_____ 12. Careers in _____ _____ include many kinds of tasks such as renting and managing property for clients, making appraisals on property, and arranging loans for home buyers.

_____ 13. _____ _____ plan and supervise the design and arrangement of building interiors and furnishings.

_____ 14. _____ companies that supply electricity, gas, and telephone services offer job opportunities related to housing.

_____ 15. Architects, engineers, and interior decorators are a few of the people with _____-level positions.

_____ 16. A(n) _____ is a person who is going through an organized program of job training that is coupled with vocational classes.

_____ 17. A(n) _____ education program offers opportunities to work part-time and attend class part-time.

(Continued)

_____ 18. A person who starts and runs his or her own housing-related business is an _____.

_____ 19. When the jobs in a career cluster are stacked according to the qualifications they require, they form a career _____ which shows the steps from entry level to professional jobs.

_____ 20. A career _____ shows that you can move in more than one direction as you change jobs within a career cluster.

_____ 21. You become _____ for a job by learning job skills.

_____ 22. The ability to guide and motivate others on the job is called _____.

_____ 23. The physical surroundings of the workplace, the work schedule, and the fringe benefits are part of the _____ _____ of a job.

_____ 24. Careers affect your _____ by determining where you live, when you have free time, and even the friendships you form.

_____ 25. When both parents are employed, the family is called _____-_____.